Housing in America

THE BABY BOOMERS TURN 65

JOHN K. McILWAIN

Urban Land Institute
Terwilliger Center for Housing

ULI Foundation

Urban Land Institute

1025 Thomas Jefferson Street, NW, Suite 500 West

Washington, DC 20007-5201

Recommended Bibliographic Listing:

McIlwain, John. *Housing in America: The Baby Boomers Turn 65.* Washington, D.C.: Urban Land Institute, 2012.

International Standard Book Number: 978-087420-219-9

About ULI

The mission of the Urban Land Institute is to provide leadership in the responsible use of land and in creating and sustaining thriving communities worldwide. ULI is committed to

- Bringing together leaders from across the fields of real estate and land use policy to exchange best practices and serve community needs;
- Fostering collaboration within and beyond ULI's membership through mentoring, dialogue, and problem solving;
- Exploring issues of urbanization, conservation, regeneration, land use, capital formation, and sustainable development;
- Advancing land use policies and design practices that respect the uniqueness of both build and natural environments;
- Sharing knowledge through education, applied research, publishing, and electronic media; and
- Sustaining a diverse global network of local practice and advisory efforts that address current and future challenges.

Established in 1936, the Institute today has nearly 30,000 members worldwide, representing the entire spectrum of the land use and development disciplines. ULI relies heavily on the experience of its members. It is through member involvement and information resources that ULI has been able to set standards of excellence in development practice. The Institute has long been recognized as one of the world's most respected and widely quoted sources of objective information on urban planning, growth, and development.

ULI Urban Land Institute

ULI SENIOR EXECUTIVES

Patrick Phillips
Chief Executive Officer

Cheryl Cummins
Executive Officer

Michael Terseck
Chief Financial Officer/Chief Administrative Officer

Richard M. Rosan
President, ULI Foundation

Joe Montgomery
Chief Executive, Europe

David Howard
Executive Vice President, Development and ULI Foundation

Lela Agnew
Executive Vice President, Communications

Marilee Utter
Executive Vice President, District Councils

ULI PROJECT STAFF

John K. McIlwain
Senior Resident Fellow
ULI/J. Ronald Terwilliger Chair for Housing

Uwe S. Brandes
Senior Vice President, Initiatives

Maureen McAvey
Senior Resident Fellow
ULI/Bucksbaum Family Chair for Retail

Lynn Ross
Executive Director, ULI Terwilliger Center for Housing

Sarah Nemecek
Research Associate

ULI PRODUCTION STAFF

James Mulligan
Senior Editor

Laura Glassman, Publications Professionals LLC
Manuscript Editor

Betsy VanBuskirk
Creative Director

John Hall Design Group
www.johnhalldesign.com
Design and Production

Craig Chapman
Senior Director, Publishing Operations

About the ULI Foundation

The ULI Foundation is the philanthropic partner of the Urban Land Institute, providing an assured source of funding for ULI's core research, education, and public service activities. Through its various giving programs, the Foundation helps strengthen ULI's ability to provide leadership in the responsible use of land to enhance the total environment.

The ULI Foundation is proud to support the ULI Fellows program by providing endowed resources made possible through the generosity of the following ULI Foundation Governors.

John Bucksbaum
Matthew Bucksbaum
Joseph C. Canizaro
Harry Frampton
James Klingbeil
Peter Rummell
J. Ronald Terwilliger

ULI Foundation

The ULI Foundation would like to recognize the following individuals for their generous philanthropy in supporting the mission of the Urban Land Institute to provide leadership in the responsible use of land.

Benefactors of the ULI Foundation

John L. Bucksbaum
Matthew Bucksbaum
Joseph C. Canizaro
Gerald D. Hines
James D. Klingbeil
Daniel Rose
J. Ronald Terwilliger

Sustainers of the ULI Foundation

Stephen W. Chamberlin
Susan C. Chamberlin
James J. Curtis
Stan Ross

Developers of the ULI Foundation

Douglas D. Abbey
Charles E. Cobb
Bruce H. Etkin
Harry H. Frampton
Lizanne Galbreath
Greenlaw Grupe
John S. Hagestad
Michael L. Horst
Charles B. Leitner
Bowen H. "Buzz" McCoy
Robert B. McLeod
Masud R. Mehran
Ronald C. Nahas
Jon Q. Reynolds
Peter S. Rummell
James W. Todd
Greg J. Vogel

Builders of the ULI Foundation

Toni Alexander
Mahlon Apgar
Joseph F. Azrack
Preston Butcher
James M. DeFrancia
Rosalind E. Gorin
James R. Harris
Gadi Kaufmann
Mark C. Kehke
Frederick A. Kober
Anthony E. Mansour
Francis Najafi
Jerome L. Rappaport
Michael T. Schueler
Geoffrey L. Stack
Thomas W. Toomey
Frank M. Transue

About the ULI Terwilliger Center for Housing

The mission of the ULI Terwilliger Center for Housing is to expand housing opportunity by leveraging the private sector and other partners to create and sustain mixed-income, mixed-use urban and suburban neighborhoods that incorporate a full spectrum of housing choices, including workforce housing, compact design, and connections to jobs, transit, services, and education. The Center achieves its mission through a multifaceted program of work that includes conducting research, publishing, convening thought leaders on housing issues, and recognizing best practices that support the mission of the Center.

Established in 2007 by J. Ronald Terwilliger, former chairman of Trammell Crow Residential, the Center's original mission was to expand the availability of workforce housing opportunities for families earning 60 to 120 percent of area median income.

Although the Center's primary focus remains on housing affordability, with a particular emphasis on workforce housing, the expanded mission now includes a broader range of housing issues. This expanded focus will integrate ULI's many housing efforts into a coherent program of work that furthers the development of mixed-income, mixed-use communities and a full spectrum of housing affordable to all, a critical aspect of ULI's core mission of the "responsible use of land."

Urban Land Institute
Terwilliger Center for Housing

Contents

A Note about Nomenclature

Today, a lot of attention is focused on the increasing population of people 65 and older in the United States, particularly the 8,000 members of the baby boom generation who will turn 65 every day for the rest of the decade. Unfortunately, discussion of the attitudes, desires, and needs of Americans over 65, and the housing markets they create, is greatly confused by a tendency to consider everyone over 65 a "senior."

This is not surprising when terms like "senior citizen," "senior vote," "senior housing," and the dreaded "senior moment" permeate the language. The Merriam-Webster dictionary, for instance, defines a "senior citizen" as "an elderly person; especially: one who has retired," a definition that certainly reflects what many Americans imagine someone over 65 to be.

But this definition simply no longer reflects the case today, and this image no longer fits many of those over 65. As in any important discussion, it is essential to understand who is being referred to, and those 65 and older today comprise three very distinct and quite different generations. This focus on terminology is not simply a matter of semantics or an effort at political correctness; rather it is recognition of the broad diversity of people who are now 65 and over, and all those who will reach 65 over the course of the decade.

To repeat, today there is no longer a single "senior" generation in America. To refer to or consider it as such is to overlook the very significant distinctions and realities that shape lives and drive markets.

Indeed, for many who are 65 and older the term "senior" is not only irrelevant, it is pejorative—and part of a growing and destructive culture of ageism. Sensitivity to the way we speak and think about those over 65 has the potential to result in a more civil society; better, thriving communities; and more relevant public policy. And, most important to the housing industry, the result will be a far better appreciation of the many dynamic and growing housing markets these generations create. For this reason, this report either refers to the three generations specifically or uses the term "65 plus" or a similar term instead of the misleading term "senior" (whenever possible).

Although the edges of these three generations overlap in their tastes, experiences, desires, and activities, they are in general as follows:

- The leading edge of the baby boom generation ("Leading-Edge Boomers"),[1] 39.8 million people born from 1946 to 1956 and now 56 to 66 years of age (the first of the 74 million members of the entire baby boom generation that was born from 1946 to 1964);[2]
- The "Greatest Generation,"[3] born from 1901 to 1927, 4.5 million people now 85 years of age and older, who grew up during the Great Depression and fought in World War II;[4] and
- In between these two groups, the "Silent Generation,"[5] 27.6 million people born from 1928 to 1945 and now 67 to 84, who grew up during the late 1940s and 1950s.[6]

Those turning 65 now and for the rest of the decade, the Leading-Edge Boomers, and many of the Silent Generation as well do not consider themselves to be "seniors" and are in fact offended by the use of this term to refer to them. They are unlike any group of individuals who have reached 65 before.

This report looks at the housing markets of these three generations from each of their perspectives, because each has its own quite distinct market, and only by looking at each is it possible to understand them. Looking across the three generations over the course of the coming decade also enables us to see the dynamism in the housing markets for those over 65 and how the progress of each generation during the decade will bring new opportunities and new challenges to the different housing industries that serve them.

Preface

Never before in the history of the United States, or of the world for that matter, have so many people been older than 65. Nor have so many of them been so healthy and active or likely to live so long. This is just the beginning; the U.S. population older than 65 will expand by over one-third this decade, causing a dramatic shift in the makeup of the American population. The implications are profound and only now beginning to be appreciated.

Driving much of this change is the demographic group known as the baby boomers, the leading edge of which is now entering their late 60s. They have been a generation that has challenged and changed the world about them for better or worse since they began entering adulthood in the late 1960s. To look at them today—healthier, more energetic, and with years of active life ahead—is to see a new stage of life emerging. In the decade ahead few of them will be retiring in traditional ways; they are instead entering a new stage that the cultural anthropologist Mary Catherine Bateson calls "Adulthood II." What they will do, how they will do it, and where they will do it are impossible to predict, except to say that it will not be what prior generations have done. Most likely they will pursue a variety of courses, disrupt expectations, create new opportunities, and present new challenges.

All of this is affecting the housing industry at a time when it is still struggling with the hangover of the Great Recession. To help the housing industry, as well as politicians and policy makers at all levels, better understand the opportunities for the industry—and the challenges—this report explores the following major themes:

- What are the characteristics of the three generations that comprise the 65-plus population today, and how will they change in the decade ahead?
- Where have they been relocating, and where are they likely to move in the future?
- What will be the impact of the distinct cultural, economic, and health differences among the three distinct age groups:
  - The Leading-Edge Boomers (now 56 to 66);
  - The Greatest Generation, now 85 plus; and
  - The Silent Generation, now 67 to 84.
- What is the effect on the suburbs of the increasing number of people in the Greatest and Silent generations choosing to age in place?
- How are central cities and town centers being developed in the suburbs meeting the needs of the member of the Greatest and Silent generations who are choosing the amenities and conveniences of a more urban, walkable lifestyle?
- When will those in the Silent Generation decide to move into traditional housing communities for seniors, and what will attract them to these communities, or will they instead find ways to age in place?
- What are some of the new markets that are opening up as the Leading-Edge Boomers and members of the Silent Generation explore new ways of living, and which trends are significant?

The fundamental point to take away from this report is that each of the generations now 65 plus differs and has distinct housing needs and markets. The opportunities these generations present for the housing industry can be understood only by looking at each one and by recognizing that the future of the housing markets for each will be unlike those of past markets for people in their age group.

Another important point is that no level of government is ready for the challenge these generations present as they live longer than prior generations, all too often outliving their savings. Inevitably pressure will grow on the resources of the federal government to provide additional support to ensure a healthy and dignified retirement.

This pressure will come as the members of generation Y, now in their 20s and early 30s—a generation more numerous than even the baby boomers—face the worst economic situation of any young generation since the Great Depression. How the competing needs among generations will be met will be one of the defining political debates of the coming decade and beyond.

It is hoped that this report can contribute to a better understanding of these issues, as well as offer ways the housing industry and localities can better meet the needs of each of the three over-65 generations.

Acknowledgments

The author would like to thank fellow ULI senior fellows Tom Murphy and Maureen McAvey for invaluable suggestions, insights, and encouragement. Aaron Conley, vice chairman of ULI's Senior Housing Council and president and managing principal of Third Act Solutions, a senior housing development company, offered excellent advice. Other industry experts did as well. Sarah Nemecek has provided help in numerous ways, including analysis of U.S. census and other data. Judy Holbrook undertook the onerous task of reviewing an early draft of this paper and offering helpful insights and support. Finally, my wife, Wende McIlwain, reviewed, commented on, and edited the final drafts, greatly improving the report. Thanks also go to all the ULI staff whose skill and hard work made this report possible. It should go without saying that all of these people, so kind and generous with their time and insights, share credit for whatever value the report may have; only the author is responsible for the report's shortcomings and errors.

The views and opinions expressed in this report are the author's and do not represent the views of the Urban Land Institute. And as is always the case where a report makes predictions about the future in a field that is changing rapidly, no certainty exists that the future will unfold as predicted here; as Yogi Berra is reported to have said, it is very hard to make predictions, especially about the future.

Introduction and Executive Summary

The rapid and unprecedented increase of the number of people over 65 in the United States is frequently in the news. It has captured the attention of the press as well as of planners, politicians, and policy makers, who see challenges ahead for supporting the generations 65 and older at a time of limited resources and longer lives. The housing industry is also paying close attention as this emerging reality presents new opportunities and needs.

The great majority of those over 65 in 2012, as this report is written, are the Greatest Generation, now 85 and older, and the Silent Generation, now 67 to 84 years of age. Entering this age group in increasing numbers each year are the members of the Leading-Edge Boomers, those baby boomers born between 1946 and 1956, now 56 to 66 years of age.

The 40 million Leading-Edge Boomers are a unique group, one that has disrupted past patterns and challenged past ideas and ways of doing things. They have healthier bodies and more energy today than any generation their age in history and are expected to be active and productive for many years to come. Their views on this stage of life are new and evolving—and are creating unexpected market opportunities.

Some who have been in the housing business for years doubt that the Leading-Edge Boomers actually will age differently from prior generations; an aging body, they say, is an aging body no matter what generation. They may be right, and it is never wise to totally discount the voice of experience.

Bearing this caution in mind, one must consider that periods exist when cultures, and the markets they affect, shift profoundly and discontinuities occur. The present is such a time in the United States. The combination of the particular culture and experience of the boomers, their extraordinary health and energy, and the stress of the current economic crisis is a volatile mix likely to produce new and innovative ways of living and significant market opportunities for those who pay close attention to rapidly emerging trends.

What this means for housing is that the past cannot be relied upon as an adequate predictor of the future. Perhaps physical changes in the bodies of the boomers will finally dampen their exploratory and pioneering spirit; if so, it will occur at a significantly later age than for any prior generation. That alone means another decade or more will pass before they settle into a quiet retirement and decide to move into traditional housing communities for seniors. Even then, what they will want is likely to be quite different from what today's housing communities for seniors provide, or they may instead find new ways to obtain the support they need to stay in their homes and age in place.

This is all part of a major global demographic shift, as those over 60 become a larger percentage of the world's population. Over 11 percent of the world's population today is older than 60 and this percentage is projected to grow to 20 percent by the end of the decade.

Some countries are facing greater challenges in this regard than others, two of which are China and Japan. China's population continues to grow, but the one-child policy is changing the makeup of the population; it is a developing country whose long-term prospects will be challenged by the changing balance between the young and those over 60. Japan, in contrast, is an extreme example of the many developed countries whose population is declining while its 60-plus population is increasing, leading to acute challenges in the years ahead.

By global standards, the United States has a relatively young population, especially for a developed country, though its 65-plus population is growing at an accelerating pace. Today the members of the Silent and the Greatest generations, who constitute most of the 65-plus population, are mostly married, white homeowners and generally wealthier than the rest of the population. They have higher incomes and a lower poverty rate than any group of this age in the past. Although they are better educated than prior generations, they are less well educated than the generations that follow them.

The members of the Leading-Edge Boomers are also overwhelmingly white, married, and homeowners. They will work longer than the generations preceding them; already more in this group are working today than at any time over the past 30 years. In the years ahead the Leading-Edge Boomers will have better health and more energy than even the Silent and Greatest generations, and they can expect an even longer life. In contrast, the Leading-Edge Boomers have less saved for retirement and a greater debt load than the two generations preceding them. Only some of them have the funds to retire comfortably for the long lives ahead of them.

During the last decade (or at least the early part of it), the members of the Silent and Greatest generations moved from the cold northeast and old industrial metropolitan regions to warmer climes in the south, west, and southwest, a migration widely noted by many commentators. Yet not all metropolitan regions or cities in the south and west saw their 65-plus population grow.

This migration south and west slowed noticeably after the start of the recession. Fewer of the Leading-Edge Boomers may make as many similar moves this coming decade. Considerable disagreement exists about this possibility, but the housing bust has trapped many Leading-Edge Boomers in large suburban homes whose values have fallen, often below the amount of debt they secure. Even those willing and able to sell their homes are likely to be more conservative, more risk averse, and so less willing to head off to new horizons in the face of an uncertain economy. Many will stay where they are today, while many others will move along many divergent paths.

Those 67 years of age and older, the Silent and Greatest generations, are significantly affecting the communities where their numbers are increasing fastest. Those who are not moving and are staying in their suburban homes are also changing the nature of these communities, creating "naturally occurring retirement communities," or NORCs. This transition is presenting new challenges to local governments and new responses about how to meet these generations' needs in places designed for young families with children and cars. Local politics are changing in response to the often more conservative views of these generations; what they want and will vote for are services more geared to their needs, such as parks, libraries, and centers for seniors instead of the schools and athletic facilities that serve families with children.

Much has also been written about the empty-nester phenomenon, namely those Leading-Edge Boomers in their late 50s and early 60s who have sold their suburban homes after their children moved out and bought a condominium or townhouse in the city. The trend is real though hard to quantify. Urban living is no longer confined to the central city; growing numbers of suburban town centers are developing around the country to which people of all ages are moving, a trend not captured by the census.

Today, more than 12 million people older than 80 constitute the Greatest Generation and the older members of the Silent Generation. This group will grow by 2.4 million to 4 million this decade, depending on the increase in life expectancy over the period, and represents a growth of 20 percent or more in the market for housing communities for seniors. Despite this growth, the industry is struggling to attract the members of the Silent Generation and to keep its communities filled. As a result, the average age of new residents is rising and is now 84.

Several causes for this are possible. Among them are the concern of many members of the Silent Generation about the cost of housing communities for seniors and their wish to preserve limited retirement funds as long as possible. This generation also displays a growing antipathy to institutional living, expressed in the desire to age in place. Attracting members of the Silent Generation to these communities has become harder, a challenge likely to be even greater when the even more independent Leading-Edge Boomers reach their late 70s in ten years.

Today the Silent Generation and the Leading-Edge Boomers, people in their late 50s through their early 80s, are already exploring a variety of differing living situations, such as cohousing, college towns, and multigenerational living. Some of these formats will survive whereas others may be shorter lived. Given the large number of people in these two generations, however, each new way of living can present a real and viable market for a developer close enough to consumers to really understand their desires.

During this decade, governments must play a growing role in providing for the housing of the Silent and Greatest generations, a role that varies at different levels. State and local governments, among other things, are closely involved in the regulation of housing communities for seniors and need to review and streamline their regulations to reduce the cost of housing as much as is reasonable and responsible. The federal government, in addition to providing general oversight over the quality of care for those living in housing communities for seniors, is also the funder of last resort.

The fact is that many members of all three generations will be financially challenged in the decade ahead. The pressure will grow on the federal government to provide for the needs of all three generations. It will, however, come into conflict with the needs of younger generations already facing intense financial pressure and uncertain futures. In the offing are all the makings of growing generational political friction.

This report provides an overview of some of the challenges and opportunities ahead for both the private housing industry and policy makers at various levels of government with the hope that it will stimulate discussion and support effective efforts to meet the needs of these generations in the years ahead.

CHAPTER 1

Three Post-65 Generations

THE LEADING-EDGE BOOMERS, THE GREATEST GENERATION, AND THE SILENT GENERATION

Not so long ago, everyone over 65 had much the same outlook on life. This has been the historical experience of aging for centuries, namely, that those over 65 represented a largely homogenous age group.

Over the course of the last two decades, however, an unprecedented change has occurred, and today three distinct generations are over 65, each with its own historical experience and with its own outlook on life generated by that history. What follows is an overview of these three 65-plus generations.

Leading-Edge Boomers

The Leading-Edge Boomers comprise the 40 million baby boomers born between 1946 and 1956, part of the 74 million baby boomers who were born during the 18 years between 1946 and 1964. This leading edge will turn 65 over the coming decade. Now 56 to 66 years of age, they have already been disrupting past patterns and challenging past ideas and ways of living and working. They are healthier and more energetic, and they expect to have a longer period of healthy, active, and productive life than any previous generation.

Will the members of the Leading-Edge Boomers act like those of the Silent and Greatest generations in the years ahead? Some experts believe they will. The experts have seen that as people reach different stages of life they respond in the same manner as those before them regardless of what they may have said in their younger years. Despite the many extraordinary circumstances

FIGURE 1 **The Nation's 55-to-64 Population Expanded by Nearly Half in the 2000s** | CHANGE IN POPULATION BY AGE GROUP, 2000–2010

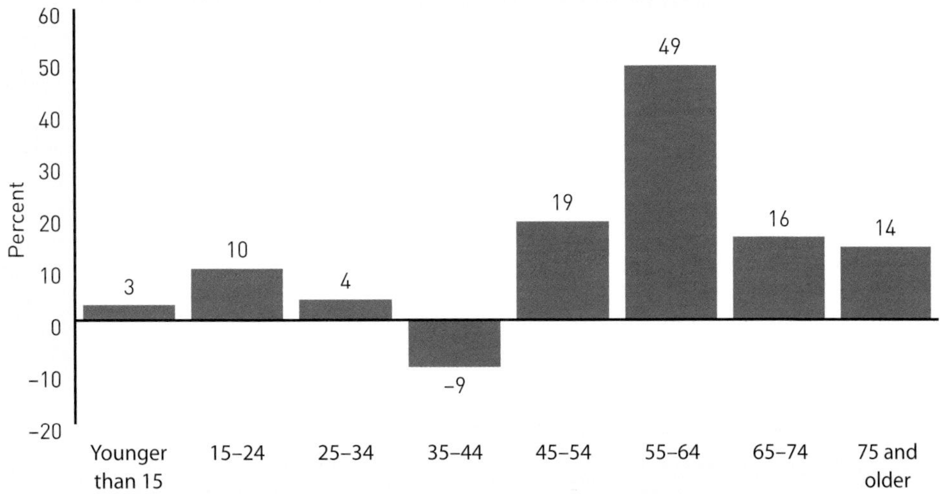

Source: Brookings Institution analysis of U.S. Census Bureau Population Estimates Program data and projections.

of the decade in which they came of age and the special characteristics of the Leading-Edge Boomers, this wisdom may be correct.

Today, however, the United States is in the midst of rapidly shifting trends and considerable economic and cultural discontinuity. The country has gone through the worst recession since the Great Depression, and the recovery is still slow and painful. Looking back one can easily see the profound changes in the country that resulted from the political and economic turmoil of the 1930s, including major changes in the role of the national government, the creation of the first national social safety net, and a cultural shift to a more sober and saving-oriented approach to life. During that decade, of course, one could not predict the nature of the changes then underway. Such is also the situation today.

This year, 2012, is the fifth year of economic turmoil in the United States and around the world, and the only thing clear is that the end of economic uncertainty is not in sight. Employment remains soft, and many of the new jobs that are being created are at flat or falling wage levels. National politics are gridlocked as the country struggles to face a weak economy and a burgeoning national debt. The uncertainty of the global economy is troubling, with the future of the euro, the second-largest global currency, at risk. The Chinese behemoth is slowing and facing internal turmoil, and the oil-rich Middle East faces ongoing instability.

Furthermore, the circumstances of aging today are unique in history. At the beginning of the last century the average life expectancy at birth in the United States was 47 years of age, and although some lived to 65, they were few, likely to be frail, and not expected to live for many more years. Today, the average life expectancy at birth is 78, and it is over 90 for most of those who reach the age of 65 healthy and who do not work in debilitating physical occupations.

These additional 31 years of expected life have not been just "tacked on at the end," according the writer and cultural anthropologist Mary Catherine Bateson;[7] she considers it instead to be a new stage of life. "Today's sixty-five year olds," she says, "are starting new careers, or continuing old ones, traveling around the world, and eloping with new loves."[8] She calls this new stage of life "Adulthood II":

> I think we need to think in terms of a first adulthood stage we can call Adulthood I, a very busy and productive time, which includes both our primary child-rearing years and the building of careers, and a new stage we can call Adulthood II. Adulthood II may begin as early as age forty (for example, for athletes whose careers may last only twenty years) and may extend past eighty (for example, for politicians, if they reach the Senate, and many self-employed people), for many years of participation and contribution. Both as individuals and as a society we are being taken by surprise by this change, yet so far most of the discussion focuses on its financial implications, not its opportunities. . . . How will the rest of life be different?[9]

Today, both the Leading-Edge Boomers and many of the members of the Silent Generation may be said to be in this stage of Adulthood II.

Surveys suggest that Leading-Edge Boomers are generally satisfied and relatively optimistic.[10] Their two biggest concerns are their health and their financial security. They continue to be physically active and are willing to replace knees and hips to continue skiing, biking, hiking, playing tennis, and picking up their grandchildren as long as possible, a period that is going to be far longer than for prior generations. Most important, they do not experience themselves as "seniors."

Although most of the Leading-Edge Boomers did move to the suburbs, following their parents, they have in many other ways broken new ground throughout their adult life. From the civil rights and antiwar protests; from birth control and rock music; from the women's and environmental movements; from ongoing political activism, drugs, and the culture of youth to today's continuing creative destruction of the high-tech sector and globalization, the Leading-Edge Boomers have brought an acceleration in the pace of change in all parts of life. As Bateson says of them:

> [They] remember their own grandparents as elderly without feeling elderly themselves. They are beginning to understand that they will not age in the same way and at the same pace, and above all that they must discover or invent new patterns for the years beyond traditional retirement, often as much as three decades, far too many years to spend on golf, television, and bridge, far too valuable to be expended on kinds of volunteerism that do not fully engage their skills or benefit from their perspectives.[11]

William H. Frey, a demographer and senior fellow at the Brookings Institution, shares Bateson's views of the distinct nature of the Leading-Edge Boomers:

> The aging of the baby boom generation is noteworthy not only because of its large size, but also because its members' social and demographic profile contrasts sharply with earlier generations at retirement age. Boomers possess more education, have more women in the labor force, are more likely to occupy professional and managerial positions, and are [somewhat] more racially and ethnically diverse than their predecessors. At the same time, their higher rates of divorce and separation, lower rates of marriage, and fewer children signal the potential for greater divisions in seniorhood between those who will live comfortably, and those who will have fewer resources available to them.[12]

Therefore, healthy Leading-Edge Boomers are unlikely to conform to past patterns as they age. In other words, the past will not be a good predictor of the future of housing or any other aspect of the world for those over 65. Perhaps physical changes in their bodies will finally dampen their exploratory and pioneering spirit; if so, it will not be for another decade or more—and at a significantly later age than any prior generation. That factor alone means Leading-Edge Boomers will not settle gracefully into a quiet retirement and decide to move into traditional seniors' housing communities for years (if they ever do). Even then, many are just as likely to want something quite different from what today's housing communities for seniors provide, or they will find ways to age in place, avoiding housing communities for seniors altogether.

The Greatest Generation

Across the cultural divide from the baby boomers is the Greatest Generation, those 4.5 million people 85 years of age and older who are the parents of the boomers. The Greatest Generation is following in the footsteps of those before them with one startling difference: they are living longer than any prior generation.

Today, more than 12 million people are over the age of 80. Depending on the extent to which the average life span increases, this number will rise by 2.4 million to 5 million by 2020, an increase of 20 to 40 percent.

Over the course of the decade most of the Greatest Generation will have significant health care needs and require an array of personal services. They also will need a way of staying connected to their community and the warmth of family and friends with whom to share time and the joys and sorrows of life.

Many, of course, enjoy the benefits of adequate retirement savings, a supportive family, or both. Too many others, unfortunately, are finding that their savings are inadequate and their families unable or unwilling to help them; in fact they may have no living family, be estranged from their family, or live far from them. They have only Medicare, Medicaid, Social Security, and local volunteer or charitable services for support.

The Silent Generation

In between the Leading-Edge Boomers and the Greatest Generation are the 28 million members of the Silent Generation, ranging from 67 years of age to the early 80s, with one foot in the culture of prior generations and one foot in culture of the boomers. ("Think Tina Turner, Mick Jagger, or Harrison Ford, all Silents," one industry expert noted.) This generation is not silent politically and has been active in national and local politics. They are a politically conservative group and were the only age group to vote for McCain in the 2008 election.

The Silent Generation has new ideas of how and where to "retire" and is acting upon them. These ideas include moving north out of Florida to Georgia, the Carolinas, and other southern states; the emergence of a small but intriguing new multigenerational cohousing movement; and affinity retirement communities (all discussed later in this report). Studying these new trends will give important clues to what the large wave of Leading-Edge Boomers may be looking for as they choose where and how to live in the years ahead.

CHAPTER 2

Changing Demographics

The international picture. The growth of the 65-plus population in the United States is part of a global demographic trend. In 2000, the global population of people 60 years of age and older was 600 million; by 2025 it is estimated to double to 1.2 billion, and by 2050 it is projected to be almost 2 billion. The proportion of the world's population older than 60 years of age is over 11 percent today and will be over 20 percent by the end of the decade.

These trends are occurring around the world, most especially among the developed countries and some of the developing nations. The population of those over 60 in the member states of the European Union is growing rapidly while at the same time the overall population in many of its states is declining. The same is true for Russia and the other members of the former Soviet Union.

Two countries in particular face especially great challenges—China and Japan—but for differing reasons. Although China's population continues to grow, the impact of the one-child policy is slowing this growth and changing the balance between those over 60 and the younger generations; it is a developing country whose long-term prospects will be challenged by this imbalance.

According to Nicolas Retsinas,[13] today 178 million Chinese are over age 60; more than 11 percent of them are over age 80. He reports that by 2050 demographers forecast that 450 million Chinese will be over age 60. As a result of the one-child policy, a child today often cares for two parents and four grandparents. This situation intensifies the need for the development of thousands of retirement homes as the cultural norm of multigenerational living is disappearing. For the great majority who cannot pay for retirement housing, the government is discussing pensions, subsidized health care, and rental subsidies.

FIGURE 2 The Population 60 Years and Older Is Expected to Increase Worldwide | DISTRIBUTION OF WORLD POPULATION 60 AND OLDER BY REGION, 2006 AND 2050

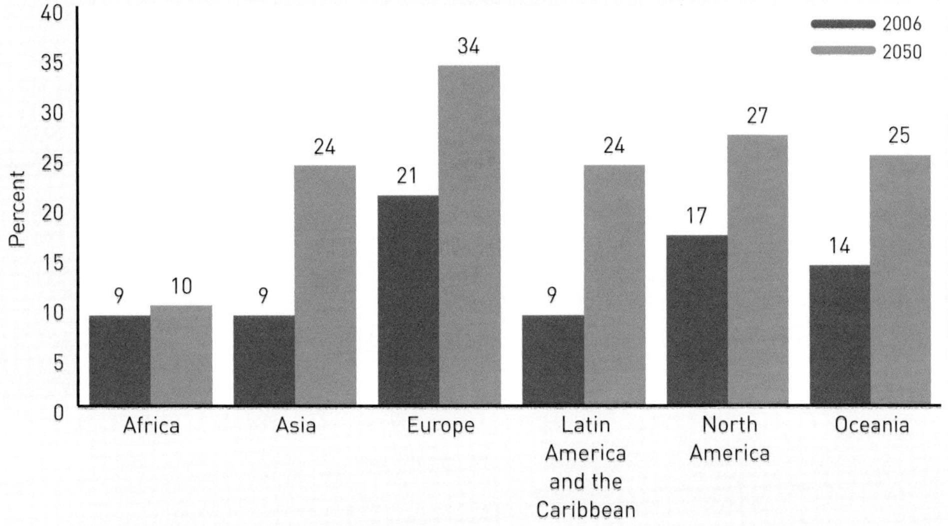

Source: United Nations Department of Economic and Socal Affairs.

Japan, in contrast, is an extreme example of the many developed countries whose populations are declining while their 65-plus population grows, potentially leading to acute challenges in the years ahead. In 2010, 23.1 million Japanese were over the age of 65, 18.0 percent of the population, the highest percentage of any country; by 2020 that number is projected to rise by 6 million to 29.2 million, 23.8 percent of the population.[14] At the same time, the country's total population is expected to decline by over 5 million. These trends are expected to accelerate in the following decades; by 2050, 40 million people 65 plus will constitute 42 percent of a population that will have fallen to 95 million. Japan faces an acute imbalance among the generations, and as a result the challenge of providing housing and care for the 65-plus generation will be a daunting prospect for a nation with a gross public debt of 235.8 percent of gross domestic product, making it the world's most indebted country.

The growing U.S. 65-plus population. Although the United States has a relatively young population, especially for a developed country, 13 percent of the population was over 65 as of the 2010 census, and the number of people in this group is projected to increase more rapidly in the future. For instance, from 1990 to 2000 the 65-plus population grew at 12 percent; for the next ten years it grew by 20 percent, reaching 40.3 million by 2010. During the current decade, recent projections by the Census Bureau[15] show the 65-plus population growing to 54.8 million,

FIGURE 3 Proportion of 65-Plus Population by Country

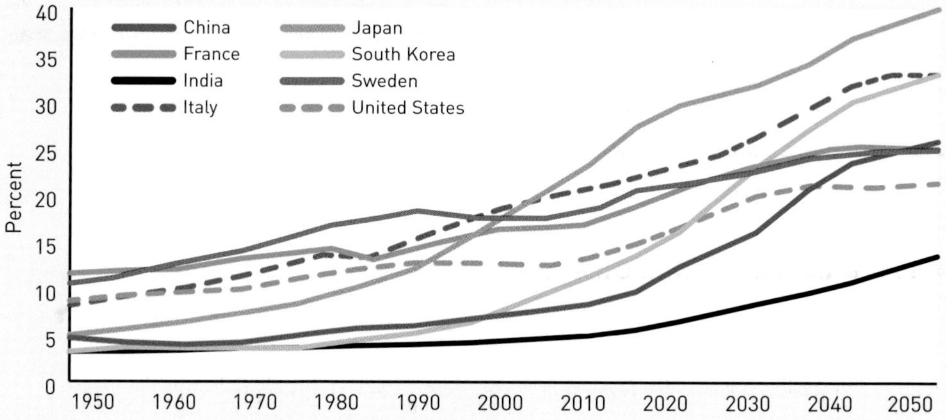

Sources: Statistics Bureau, *Statistical Handbooks of Japan 2011* (Ministry of Internal Affairs and Communications); Ministry of Health, Labour and Welfare; United Nations.

FIGURE 4 The Median Age of the American Population Will Increase by 2050 | RESIDENT POPULATION PROJECTIONS BY AGE, 2010–2050 (THOUSANDS)

	2010	**2020**	**2050**
Total population	310,233	341,387	439,010
55 years and older	76,504	97,807	136,658
65 years and older	40,229	54,804	88,547
75 years and older	18,766	22,492	48,434
85 years and older	5,751	6,597	19,041
Median age (years)	**36.9**	**37.7**	**39**

Source: U.S. Census Bureau, 2008 National Population Projections, August 2008.

a 36 percent increase. This will happen as the 40 million Leading-Edge Boomers reach 65 this decade. They, along with the Greatest and Silent generations, will live longer than prior generations: current estimates are that 64 percent of all Americans will live to 75 years of age, and 35 percent will reach 85.[16]

Ethnicity. As of 2010, 32 million, or 80 percent, of those over 65 were non-Hispanic white. The Leading-Edge Boomers, those today 56–67 years of age, are 76 percent non-Hispanic white.

FIGURE 5 The Number of 65-Plus Americans Is Projected to Grow Rapidly | POPULATION 65 YEARS AND OLDER, 1900–2050

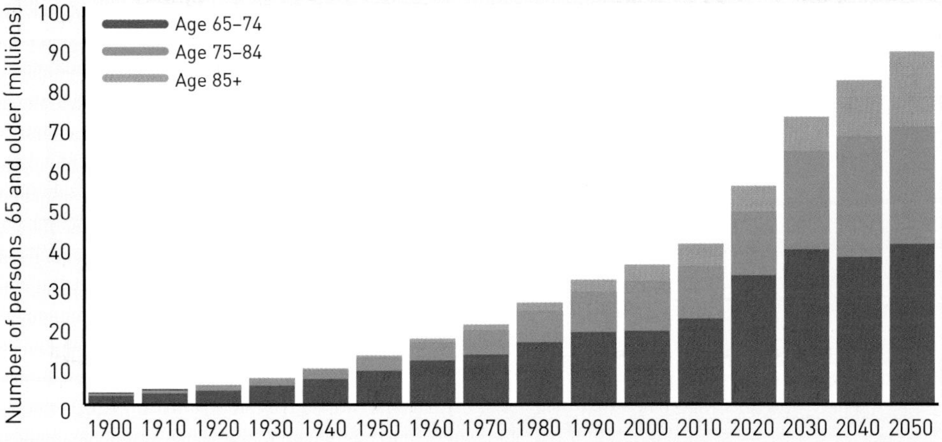

Source: U.S. Census Bureau, compiled by the U.S. Administration on Aging, 2008.

FIGURE 6 Compared with Other Age Groups, the Number of Americans 65 and Older Will Change Most Significantly | PROJECTIONS OF THE CHANGE IN POPULATION BY AGE GROUP, 2010 TO 2050

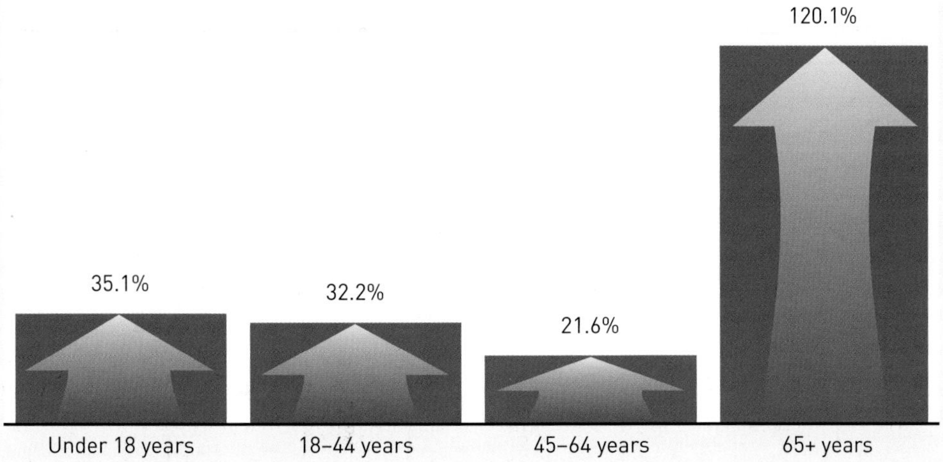

Source: U.S. Census Bureau, 2008.

FIGURE 7 **Shifting Ethnicities between U.S. Generations** | PERCENT OF POPULATION BY AGE AND ETHNICITY, 2009

Ethnicity	Silent and Greatest generations	Leading-Edge Boomers
Black	8.6%	10.5%
Asian	3.4%	4.0%
Hispanic	7.0%	8.6%
White	80.1%	75.7%

Source: U.S. Census Bureau, 2012.

FIGURE 8 **The Median Age of White Americans Is Higher Than That of Other Ethnic Groups** | MEDIAN AGE BY ETHNICITY, 2009

Group	Years
United States	36.8
Black	31.3
Asian	35.3
Hispanic	27.4
White	41.2

Source: U.S. Census Bureau, 2012.

FIGURE 9 **The U.S. 65-Plus Population Will Remain Largely Non-Hispanic White** | PERCENT OF POPULATION BY AGE AND ETHNICITY, 2000 AND 2009

Age (years)	2000	2009
Black		
5–24	15.3%	15.2%
65+	8.2%	8.6%
Asian		
5–24	3.8%	4.3%
65+	2.3%	3.4%
Hispanic		
5–24	16.7%	20.0%
65+	5.0%	7.0%
White		
5–24	62.1%	58.0%
65+	83.9%	80.1%

Source: U.S. Census Bureau, 2012.

FIGURE 10 **The Silent and Greatest Generations Possess High Homeownership Rates** | HOMEOWNERSHIP RATES BY AGE GROUP IN 2010

Age (years)	Homeownership rate
45–49	70%
50–54	75%
55–59	78%
60–64	80%
65–69	82%
70–74	82%
65+	81%
75+	79%

Source: U.S. Census Bureau, 2012.

In a country with a growing minority population, the difference among ethnicity and race between the Leading-Edge Boomers on the one hand and the Silent and Greatest generations on the other is less than between the 65-plus population as a whole and younger generations. The median age of the white population is considerably higher than that of other ethnic and racial groups and rising faster than that of the Latino, black, and Asian populations; the rapid growth in the nonwhite population is occurring among the young generations. As a result, the 65-plus population will remain largely non-Hispanic white during the coming decade while the country as a whole moves to a more diverse ethnicity.

Homeownership. The members of the Silent and Greatest generations have the highest rate of homeownership in the country, followed closely by Leading-Edge Boomers; after they reach 75 years of age, however, homeownership begins to decline. The census reports that as of 2010, when the national homeownership rate was 66 percent, the profile of homeownership by age was as shown in figure 10.

A striking fact is that despite the recession, the housing crash, and the resultant decline in the national homeownership rate from 69 percent in 2004 to 65.4 percent as of the end of the first quarter of 2012, households headed by those over 65 and Leading-Edge Boomers saw no decline in homeownership. The crisis hit younger households hardest—the younger the age group, the harder. The result, as David Leonhardt noted in a *New York Times* article on June 24, 2012, is that the difference in the homeownership rate between those over 65 and those under 35 is the greatest since the Census Bureau has been collecting these data.

Home equity. The high rate of homeownership among those over 65 has been a financial boon for them. Over the past several decades their home values have fared far better than those of younger generations. The homeowners among the Silent and Greatest generations have also been less affected by the current housing recession than younger groups, perhaps because they

FIGURE 11 **The Recession Did Not Lower Homeownership Rates of Older Americans** | HOMEOWNERSHIP RATE BY AGE OF HOUSEHOLDER, 1984, 2005, AND 2009 (%)

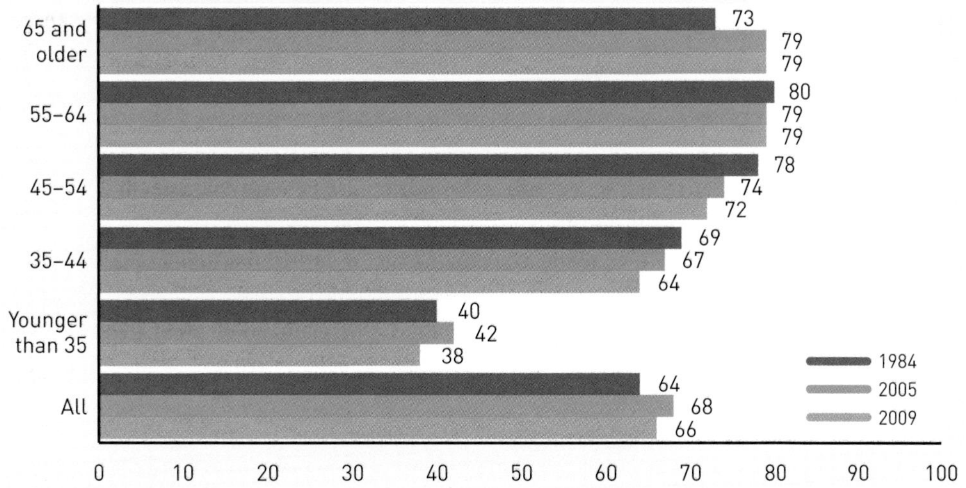

Source: Pew Research Center, 2011.

FIGURE 12 **The Home Equity of 65-Plus Americans Has Fared Better Than That of Younger Generations** | CHANGES IN MEDIAN HOME EQUITY BY AGE GROUP, 1984, 2005, AND 2009

Age group (years)	Home equity 1984	Home equity 2005	Percent change 1984–2005	Home equity 2009	Percent change 2005–2009	Percent change 1984–2009
All	$81,143	$111,685	38%	$87,420	−22%	8%
Younger than 35	$35,150	$50,258	43%	$24,396	−51%	−31%
55–64	$108,051	$139,606	29%	$114,864	−18%	6%
Older than 65	**$92,336**	**$156,359**	**69%**	**$145,361**	**−7%**	**57%**

Source: Pew Research Center, 2011.

have been living in more established neighborhoods that have seen values decline less. As a result of this, and due also, perhaps, to a more conservative approach to paying off their mortgages, as discussed below, the median home equity of those over 65 has increased 57 percent from 1984 to 2009.

Not all generations have benefited equally from a rise in home equity. Studying figure 12, which compares the home equity trends of several age cohorts from 1984 to 2009, indicates the following:

- Over this period, median home equity for all homeowners increased only 8 percent, held back especially by the large 31 percent drop in median home equity among those homeowners under 35 years of age.
- The Leading-Edge Boomers, those who were then 55–64 years of age, saw only a 6 percent increase in their home equity over this period.
- Although all age groups saw a steady increase in home equity from 1984 to 2005, the trend reversed for the following five years to 2009. During those years the housing crash most heavily affected the young, whose median home equity was cut in half, while the Leading-Edge Boomers lost almost one-fifth of their median home equity. Those over 65 lost only 7 percent.

Those under 35 years of age have been especially hard hit by a combination of two factors. Because they are (or were) more recent homeowners looking for their first, starter homes, many moved to the newer, outer-edge suburbs. Many drove to the outer suburbs seeking home prices low enough for them to buy and to qualify for a mortgage. This strategy, however, exposed them to some of the worst abuses of the recent toxic mortgage scams. As a result, many of them lost their homes or at least found their homes seriously underwater, worth far less than the mortgages.

The causes and the impact of the drop in median home equity for the Leading-Edge Boomers is different and of concern. A 2005 study for the Harvard Joint Center for Housing Studies noted:

> Households reaching retirement age in the 1970s and earlier typically had paid off their mortgages as they reached mid-life. . . .
>
> In the 1980s and 1990s this pattern of paying off the mortgage by late mid-life began to change. Cohorts approaching retirement now typically still carry substantial mortgage debt.[17]

The study was based on the 2000 census, and what followed 2000 was a continued rise of housing debt among baby boomers, an increase that ended a couple of years after the publication of the Harvard Joint Center paper. In what proved to be an overly optimistic assessment, the paper noted:

> The cohort housing debt trends we have just described need not raise any red flags if increasing housing debt is matched by equally large or larger increases in the value of the homes being purchased, if these values hold up in the future, and if the investment in housing that the debt has secured remains relatively liquid.[18]

Unfortunately, housing values tumbled and housing has not remained liquid. Although most of the boomers live in well-established communities that have fared better than others, many were among those described in the Harvard study who aggressively refinanced and took out home equity loans as their homes increased in value until 2007. Consequently, they have significantly less equity in their homes than homeowners in the Silent and Greatest generations and will continue to carry high levels of mortgage debt in the years ahead. Therefore, the Leading-Edge Boomers are less financially prepared than the Silent and Greatest generations and will have to defer retirement, which is just what is occurring.

Employment. More members of the Leading-Edge Boomers are in fact working today than any in this age group over the past 30 years. Nationally the number of workers over 55 rose 12 percent between 2007, the start of the recession, and 2011. During the same period, the number of workers 25–54 years of age fell by 7 percent. Joseph de Avila reported in the *Wall Street Journal* on March 27, 2012, that the unemployment rate for those over 55 was only 5.9 percent compared to the overall unemployment rate of 8.3 percent.[19]

Studies of Leading-Edge Boomers by the AARP indicate that around 70 percent of boomers say they intend to work past traditional retirement age. One obvious reason for this decision is their concern about financial security. As they review their retirement plans, many discover that their current life expectancy is far longer than they thought or planned for. Happy as they may be about this outcome, it raises the fear that their retirement funds, often depleted by the recession, may be inadequate and that they need to keep working. Working longer is both a benefit to them (and to a society that can reap the advantage of their experience and wisdom) and a challenge; can they at this late stage build sufficient savings to live the life in retirement they had planned?

FIGURE 13 More Leading-Edge Boomers Are Working Today Than over the Past 30 Years | SHARE OF POPULATION EMPLOYED, AGE 65 AND OLDER, 1967–2010

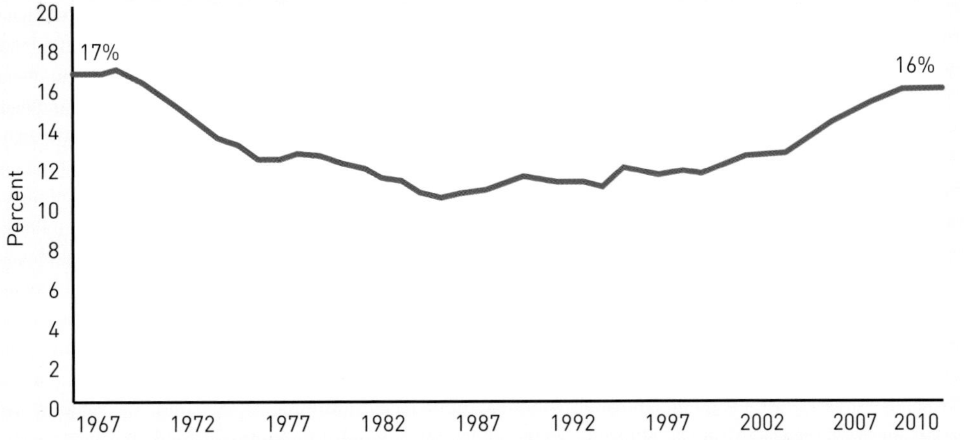

Source: Pew Research Center analysis of Bureau of Labor Statistics data.

FIGURE 14 During the Recession, Americans over Age 55 Experienced a Positive Change in Employment | EMPLOYMENT CHANGES BY AGE GROUPS, 2007:Q4–2009:Q3

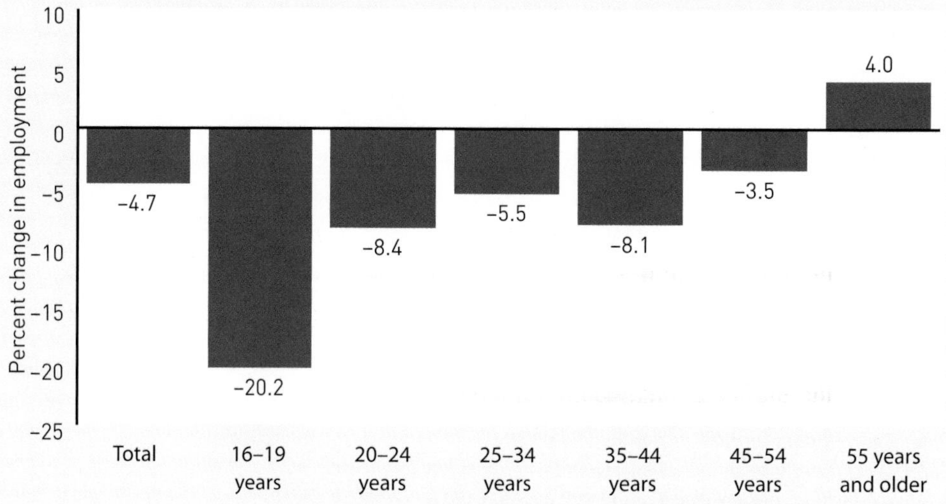

Source: Kristie M. Engemann and Howard J. Wall, "The Effects of Recessions across Demographic Groups," *Federal Reserve Bank of St. Louis Review* (January/February 2010).

Income. Understandably, the median income of those older than 65 is lower than that of younger age groups. Recently, however, the difference between their income and that of those 35 and younger has been narrowing considerably.

As figure 15 from the Pew Research Center[20] shows, the difference between the household incomes of those under 35 and those over 65 converged from 1965 to 2010. Reasons for the convergence include the high unemployment rate of younger people, the gradual decline in all wages, and the rising number of those 65 plus continuing to work.

Some 55 percent of the income of households headed by those over 65 comes from Social Security; this share has held steady the past several decades. The share of their income from wages and salaries, however, increased from 14 percent in 2000 to 17 percent in 2010.

Although the incomes of all those over 65 have been rising, the burden of housing costs increases with age, perhaps as incomes decline. According to the Center for Housing Policy, 25 percent of households headed by a member of the Greatest Generation, someone over 85, pay at least half their income for housing, compared with about 20 percent for households headed by someone 65–74 years of age and about 17 percent for households with a head younger than 65.[21]

Wealth. Although the income of those over 65 is still less than that of younger households, unsurprisingly their wealth is greater. The difference between their wealth and that of young households has been widening dramatically, according to a Pew Research Center analysis of census data.[22] It reports that from 1984 to 2009, the difference in net worth between these two age groups grew from 10:1 to 47:1. As David Leonhardt notes in a *New York Times* article on June 24, 2012, this gap is wider than at any time since the Federal Reserve began keeping these data consistently in 1989.

The causes of this striking shift in wealth are varied, including but not limited to the recent recession that, like all recessions, hit those starting out far harder than those already established. According to the Pew Research Center report, other long-term changes have also occurred, including starting work and marrying at later ages, as well as carrying higher college debt.[23]

FIGURE 15 **Incomes of Americans over 65 Have Changed Dramatically since 1967** | CHANGE IN MEDIAN ADJUSTED HOUSEHOLD INCOME BY AGE OF HOUSEHOLDER, 1967–2010 (%)

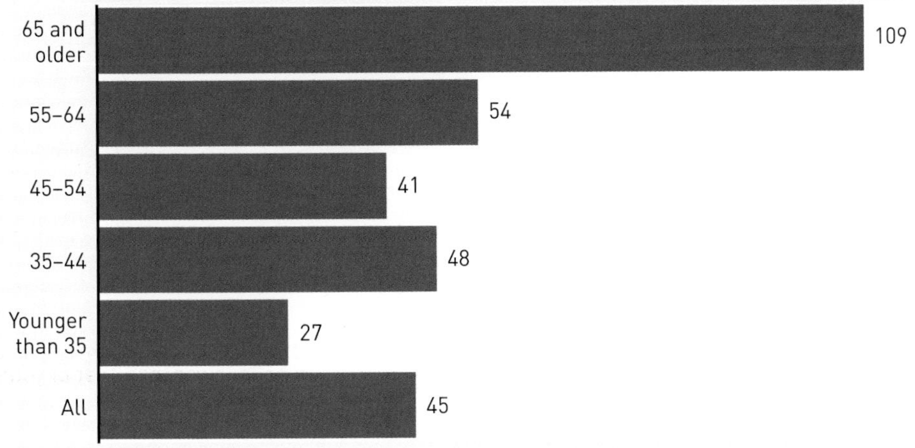

Source: Pew Research Center, 2011.
Note: Standardized to 2010 dollars and a household size of three.

FIGURE 16 **Income of Americans 65 and Older and Younger Than 35 Is Converging** | MEDIAN ADJUSTED HOUSEHOLD INCOME BY AGE OF HOUSEHOLDER, 1967–2010

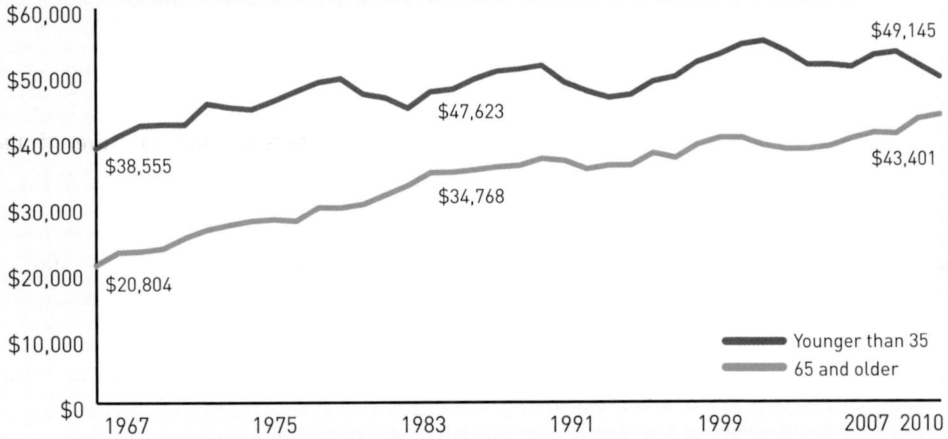

Source: Pew Research Center, 2011.
Note: Standardized to 2010 dollars and a household size of three.

FIGURE 17 **The Age Gap in Household Net Worth Is Rising** | MEDIAN NET WORTH BY AGE OF HOUSEHOLDER, 1984 AND 2009 (2010 DOLLARS)

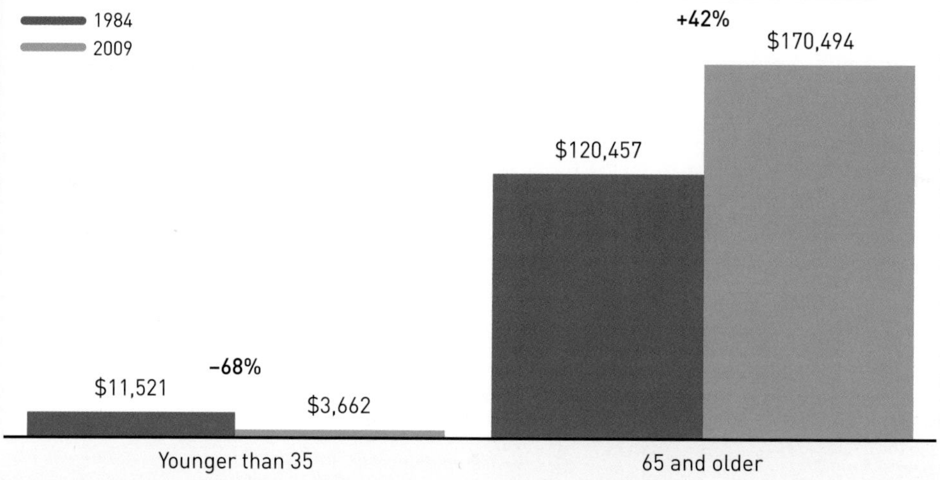

Source: Pew Research Center, 2011.

FIGURE 18 **Home Equity Represents a Larger Portion of Total Wealth in 2009 Than in 1984 for Those 65 and Older, Less for Those Under 35** | MEDIAN NET WORTH EXCLUDING HOME EQUITY OF HOUSEHOLDER, 1984 AND 2009 (2010 DOLLARS)

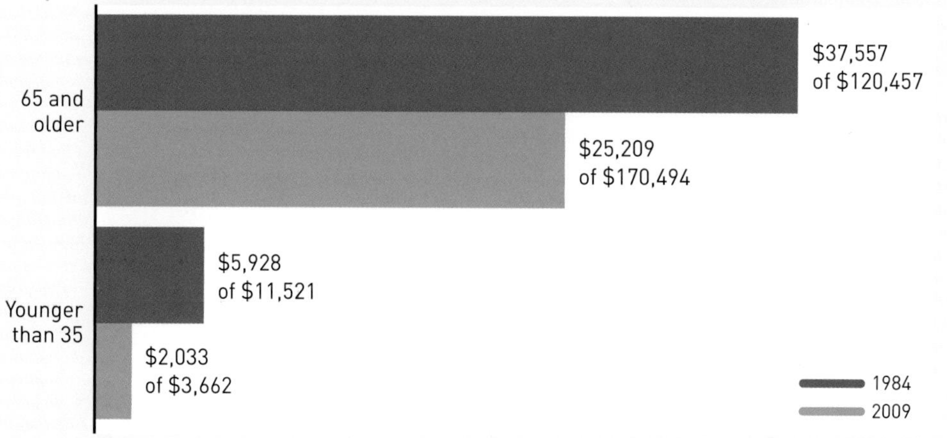

Source: Pew Research Center, 2011.

Poverty. The rate of poverty among households headed by someone 65 plus has also decreased dramatically, according to the Pew report.[24] This began with the advent of the Great Society programs during the late 1960s and 1970s. Thereafter the rate has continued to decline, albeit slowly, until only 11 percent were poor in 2010.

In contrast, poverty rates for households headed by adults younger than 35 began climbing in the 1980s and today are notably higher than they were in 1967. Among households headed by those under 35, 22 percent were in poverty in 2010, compared with 12 percent in 1967.

FIGURE 19 Homes, Rental Properties, and Real Estate Contribute the Most to the Net Worth of Those 65 and Older | MEDIAN NET WORTH BY TYPE OF ASSET AND AGE OF HOUSEHOLDER, 2009 (2010 DOLLARS)

	All	Younger than 35	35–44	45–54	55–64	65 and older
Homeownership	$ 87,420	$24,396	$ 50,825	$ 86,402	$114,864	$145,361
Rental property	121,981	71,156	101,651	111,308	152,476	172,806
Other real estate	81,321	30,495	76,238	76,238	101,651	91,486
Stocks and mutual funds	26,226	6,099	20,330	23,380	40,660	54,282
IRA and Keogh accounts	30,119	8,132	20,330	30,495	41,575	50,825
401(k) and thrift accounts	28,462	10,165	24,396	39,136	44,320	50,825
Financial institution accounts	3,863	1,525	2,440	3,863	6,201	8,132
U.S. savings bonds	1,017	508	813	1,017	1,017	1,169
Other interest-earning assets	32,528	16,801	10,416	20,330	40,660	50,825
Regular checking accounts	813	712	712	813	1,017	1,017
Business equity	25,413	15,248	20,737	25,413	30,495	28,666
Vehicles	5,301	3,154	4,778	6,353	6,793	6,277
Other assets	32,528	2,033	23,380	26,480	45,743	50,825
Unsecured liabilities	8,132	9,713	9,555	9,149	7,116	3,304

Source: Pew Research Center, 2011.

Note: Based on households that own a given asset. "Other assets" include mortgages of real estate held for sale, amounts due from sale of business property, and other financial assets.

FIGURE 20 Since 1967 the Rate of Older Americans in Poverty Has Dramatically Decreased | SHARE OF HOUSEHOLDS IN POVERTY BY AGE OF HOUSEHOLDER, 1967–2010

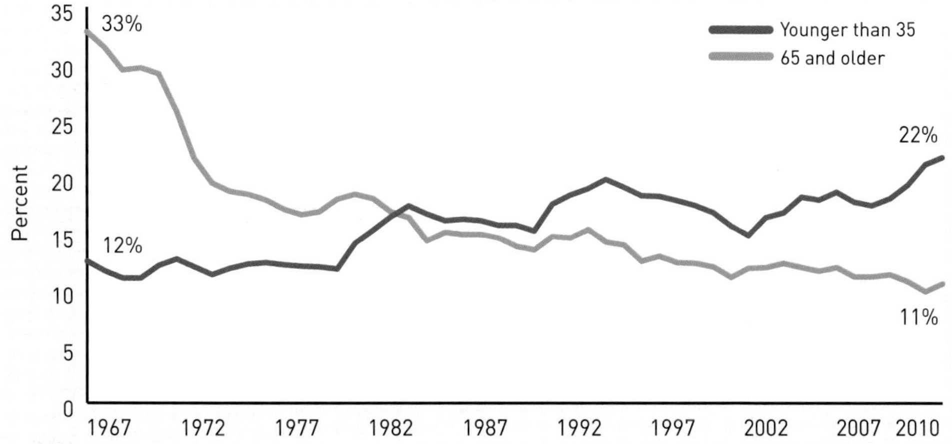

Source: Pew Research Center, 2011.

FIGURE 21 Leading-Edge Boomers Earn a Higher Percentage of Bachelor's Degrees Than Older Generations | BACHELOR'S DEGREE BY AGE, 2011

Age (years)	Percent of age group
55–59	19%
60–64	18%
65–69	15%
70–74	13%
75+	11%

Source: U.S. Census Bureau, 2011.

Education. The Leading-Edge Boomers have more members with bachelor's degrees than the Silent or Greatest generations. Of those over the age of 75, 11 percent have bachelor's degrees or more. This share increases to 13 to 15 percent for those 65–74 years of age. Among the Leading-Edge Boomers, however, the rate jumps to 18 to 19 percent. Despite this educational level, the Leading-Edge Boomers still lag behind the country as a whole; nationally 32 percent of adults have bachelor's degrees.

Marital status. Of those over 65, 56.4 percent were married in 2010,[25] which is little changed from the past couple of decades. What is changing somewhat is the reason those over 65 are single. The percentage of those widowed has dropped from 34 percent to 28 percent, whereas those divorced have doubled from 5 percent to 10 percent. Perhaps this means that living longer does not always mean living happily together longer. Current trends suggest that more members of the Silent Generation and the Leading-Edge Boomers may be choosing to live alone if they can afford to do so.

What emerges from these statistics is the financial challenge the three generations face in the decades ahead. For the Leading-Edge Boomers, this is particularly acute because much of their net worth was tied up in home equity, much of which has been lost to higher debt loads and collapsing housing values. Nor have the stock and bond markets made up the difference. Combine these declines with their longer life expectancy and the result is that more members of all three generations will not have the resources to support themselves through retirement.

More of the Leading-Edge Boomers are responding to this challenge by continuing to work, although some are unable or unwilling to do so. However, it is unlikely that many of them will be able to save and invest enough to cover a long retirement. This raises the question of whether resources can be found to fund a sufficient national safety net for those over 65; in other words, can the country find the political will to allocate limited resources to support these generations for their housing and health care needs?

Also emerging from these statistics is the extraordinary gap that has arisen between the financial well-being of those over 65 and the Leading-Edge Boomers, compared with that of those under 35, generation Y. This financial gap will create tensions between the generations just as the nation needs to find the resources to provide for both age groups. It will be one of the great political struggles for years to come and will make the efforts to modify Social Security, Medicare, and Medicaid even harder.

CHAPTER 3
Where Are They Moving?

Over the past couple of decades those 65 years and older, the members of the Silent and Greatest generations, have been moving around the country at a substantial pace, but not everywhere evenly; some cities and metropolitan regions have experienced dramatic growth in their 65-plus populations whereas others have seen a decline.

Among the 50 largest metropolitan regions in the United States, the rate at which the 65-plus population grew during the past decade ranged from a high of 50 percent to 60 percent to a decline of 5 percent. All the largest metro regions saw growth with three exceptions: Pittsburgh, New Orleans, and Buffalo.

Among cities, the variation was even wider. Whereas some cities also saw a growth in their 65-plus population of 50 percent to 60 percent, others saw it decline by 20 percent or more. Unlike large metropolitan regions, only somewhat more than half the cities in these regions saw a growth in the number of those older than 65 during the past decade.

The 2010 census numbers confirm that during the last decade (or at least the early part of it) those over 65 were moving from the cold northeast and older industrial metropolitan areas to warmer climes in the south, west, and southwest, a migration widely noted by many commentators. Yet not all metropolitan regions or cities in the south saw their 65-plus populations grow. The Tampa and New Orleans regions and several southern cities wound up losing members of the Silent and Greatest generations.

Where the Silent and Greatest generations and the Leading-Edge Boomers will move in the future, however, is hard to predict, because trends of the past decade are far from certain to continue. Of note, the last decade actually spans two quite distinct periods, the housing boom through 2006 and the housing bust and recession from 2007 on.

Recent census numbers confirm that the migration of retirees slowed noticeably after the start of the recession; from 2007 to 2009 the annual growth rate of retirement-destination counties fell to 1.7 percent after the recession began, down from 3.1 percent between 2000 and 2007. A growing number of retirement-destination counties, including some that saw an influx of those over-65 people during the early years of the past decade, also began losing their populations of those older than 65 after 2007.[26]

The strength of the housing boom during the early part of the decade served to obscure the impact of the recession and housing crash in the decennial census numbers. Looking ahead, the movement of those older than 65 will be slower for the rest of this decade than the 2010 census numbers reported below suggest; the housing bust has trapped many of the Leading-Edge Boomers in large suburban homes whose values have fallen below what they are willing to sell them for or are worth less than the debt they secure. Even people willing and able to sell their homes are likely to be more conservative, more risk averse, and thus less willing to head off to new horizons in the face of the uncertainty in the economy.

Where Did Retirees Move Regionally?

The following ten metropolitan regions saw the largest growth in the number of those over 65 during the period from 2000 to 2010:

- Los Angeles: 199,000;
- New York City: 167,000;
- Dallas: 153,000;
- Atlanta: 147,000;
- Houston: 144,000;
- Phoenix: 129,000;
- Washington, D.C.: 127,000;
- Riverside, California: 98,000;
- Chicago: 87,000; and
- Minneapolis: 69,000.

Absolute numbers, however, do not necessarily show where the members of the Silent and Greatest generations, those 65 plus, may be having the greatest political and market impact. That is better indicated by the rate at which this population is growing.

For instance, whereas the increase in the numbers of those over 65 in the New York City metropolitan region was the second highest in the nation, this population grew at only a 7 percent rate. Thus its impact is likely to be less than in, say, Raleigh, North Carolina, where the rate of growth was a stunning 60 percent. William Frey of the Brookings Institution reports that the metropolitan regions with the fastest-growing 65-plus populations were as shown in figure 22.[27]

FIGURE 22 U.S. Metro Areas with Fastest-Growing Senior Populations | PERCENT CHANGE IN 65-PLUS POPULATION, 2000–2010

Rank	Metropolitan area	Percent change
1	Raleigh-Cary, NC	60%
2	Austin-Round Rock, TX	53%
3	Las Vegas-Paradise, NV	50%
4	Boise City-Nampa, ID	46%
5	Atlanta-Sandy Springs-Marietta, GA	44%
6	Provo-Orem, UT	42%
7	Colorado Springs, CO	40%
8	Houston-Sugar Land-Baytown, TX	39%
9	Dallas-Fort Worth-Arlington, TX	38%
10	Charlotte-Gastonia-Concord, NC-SC	36%

Source: Brookings Institution analysis of 2000 and 2010 census data, 2011.

Some other major metropolitan regions showing a rapid increase in members of the Silent and Greatest generations, those now older than 68, during this period include the following:

- Phoenix: 33 percent;
- Denver: 32 percent;
- Orlando: 29 percent; and
- Riverside, California: 28 percent.

Only four of the metropolitan regions with the fastest rate of increase in the numbers of the Silent and Greatest generation members were also among the fastest growing in absolute numbers: Houston, Dallas, Phoenix, and Riverside, California; they clearly have been major magnets.

Regions that attracted those over 65 did so for various reasons. Among them were the presence of large universities, the moderate and affordable cost of living and housing, and warmer, more benign climates. They are also newer, fast-growing parts of the country where people may be moving to be close to their children and grandchildren who moved there looking for work.

Which Metropolitan Regions Are Experiencing Decline?

The metropolitan regions where the population of those over 65, the members of the Silent and Greatest generations, declined or grew most slowly in the past decade according to Frey's report are shown in figure 23.[28]

Other major metropolitan regions that saw the slowest growth in these populations include the following:

- Tampa: 4 percent;
- Philadelphia: 4 percent; and
- Detroit: 6 percent.

The regions with declining (or very-slow-growth) 65-plus populations are, with the exception of New Orleans and Tampa, among the old, declining industrial areas of the northeast and Midwest, with their harsher weather. They represent a past that many seem to have wished to leave behind.

FIGURE 23 U.S. Metro Areas with Slowest-Growing or Declining Senior Populations | PERCENT CHANGE IN 65-PLUS POPULATION, 2000–2010

Rank	Metropolitan area	Percent change
1	Scranton–Wilkes-Barre, PA	-7%
2	Pittsburgh, PA	-5%
3	New Orleans-Metairie-Kenner, LA	-5%
4	Buffalo-Niagara Falls, NY	-3%
5	Youngstown-Warren-Boardman, OH-PA	-2%
6	Providence-New Bedford-Fall River, RI-MA	1%
7	Cleveland-Elyria-Mentor, OH	1%
8	Springfield, MA	2%
9	Toledo, OH	3%
10	Milwaukee-Waukesha-West Allis, WI	4%

Source: Brookings Institution analysis of 2000 and 2010 census data, 2011.

The slow growth in the retiree population in the Tampa metropolitan region mirrors Miami's 8 percent rate. Florida did attract many retirees, but they moved to Orlando and Jacksonville, which saw the population older than 65 grow by 29 percent and 31 percent, respectively.

Overall, however, the rate of migration to Florida has been slowing; as Michael Sasso notes in an article in the *Tampa Tribune* on December 20, 2007, estimates suggest that the percentage of people older than 56 migrating in the United States who moved to Florida dropped from 19 percent in 2000 to 13 percent in 2006. Most likely there are a number of causes for this slowdown and for the fact that people are moving to cities farther inland, such as Jacksonville and Orlando. These might include recent hurricanes and the uncertain condition of the state's hurricane insurance fund, as well as comparative housing prices, among others. Some also believe concern about Florida's sinkholes and the high cost of housing, taxes, and property insurance may be discouraging people from moving to the state in the same numbers they did in the past.

Which Cities Are Seeing Retirees Move?

The cities, as distinguished from their metropolitan regions, that gained the most members of the Silent and Greatest generations over the past decade were, not surprisingly, all southern and western, including Raleigh, North Carolina, whose population grew by an amazing 60 percent. Not all cities in the south and west saw their populations of those over 65 grow, however.

For instance, a southern city saw the greatest decline among the Silent and Greatest generations, namely New Orleans. Its population of those over 65 declined 34 percent, far faster than the 5 percent decline in the region as a whole. New Orleans, however, is a special case. The population of New Orleans at all age levels had been declining for some time before Hurricane Katrina, and its aftermath accelerated that trend; the decline in those over 65 was at first simply a part of the exodus caused by the hurricane. Unlike younger families, however, many of those older than 65 did not have the resources of money or energy to return; thus, they settled elsewhere in the country. They are part of the great New Orleans diaspora that has depleted the traditions and culture, and the tight-knit communities, of this great city.

Other southern cities saw their populations of those over 65 decline as well, including Birmingham (–19 percent), Richmond (–13 percent), and Tampa (–8 percent). In the west, Salt Lake City's population of those over 65 declined by 12 percent, and Seattle's went down by 1 percent. In other words, a sunny or western city was not enough to attract those over 65. Other factors, such as cost, quality of life, and urban design, also affected this migration.

In some cities where the percentage of those over 65 in the population has risen, the increase was caused more by the out-migration of young adults in search of jobs. For instance, in Maine, Vermont, New Hampshire, and West Virginia, those older than 65 migrated in while at the same time large numbers of young people moved out.

How Do Cities and Their Suburbs Compare?

Every metropolitan region, with the exception of San Jose and Raleigh, saw a faster rate of growth in the 65-plus population than did the central city of that region. In fact, Atlanta's 65-plus population grew by only 2 percent whereas that of the metropolitan region grew by 44 percent.

FIGURE 24 Change in 65-Plus Population for Cities in the Top 50 Metro Areas versus Change for Metro Area | PERCENT CHANGE IN 65-PLUS POPULATION BY CITY AND METROPOLITAN AREA, 2000–2010

Decline			Growth		
	City	Metro region		City	Metro region
New Orleans	-34%	-5%	Raleigh	60%	60%
St. Louis	-26%	7%	Charlotte	30%	36%
Buffalo	-24%	-3%	Las Vegas	27%	50%
Pittsburgh	-23%	-5%	Austin	27%	53%
Cincinnati	-21%	11%	San Jose	24%	23%
Cleveland	-21%	1%	Jacksonville	18%	31%
Birmingham	-19%	9%	Phoenix	17%	33%
Milwaukee	-18%	4%	Houston	16%	39%
Detroit	-16%	6%	San Antonio	16%	27%
Baltimore	-15%	11%	Riverside	13%	28%
Providence	-15%	1%	Sacramento	13%	27%
Philadelphia	-13%	4%	Oklahoma City	13%	18%
Minneapolis	-13%	23	Dallas	13%	38%
Richmond	-13%	22%	Virginia Beach	11%	19%
Salt Lake City	-12%	25%	Los Angeles	10%	17%
Tampa	-8%	4%	Denver	10%	32%
Memphis	-6%	15%	San Diego	9%	12%
Chicago	-5%	9%	Columbus	7%	20%
Hartford	-4%	8%	Portland	6%	27%
Kansas City	-4%	15%	San Francisco	6%	13%
Seattle	-1%	20%	New York	6%	7%
Indianapolis	0%	18%	Orlando	6%	29%
Washington, DC	0%	29%	Miami	5%	8%
			Louisville	5%	14%
			Nashville	3%	37%
			Boston	2%	8%
			Atlanta	2%	44%

Source: U.S. Census Bureau, 2000 and 2010.

In those cities where the number of members of the Silent and Greatest generations declined, their numbers in the metropolitan region generally grew, sometimes quite rapidly, as in the case of Salt Lake City where the metro area's rate of growth was double that of the city. Exceptions to this trend were Pittsburgh, Buffalo, and New Orleans, where those older than 65 left both the city and the metropolitan region, though fewer left the metro region.

Over the past decade, the members of the Silent and Greatest generations have largely preferred suburbs to cities. Although southern and western cities like Las Vegas, Jacksonville, San Jose, Austin, Charlotte, and Raleigh attracted these generations, these cities really were not exceptions because each is a sprawling city with large boundaries that incorporate much of their surrounding suburbs.

Does this finding mean that all the reports of empty nesters moving to cities were wrong? No, what has happened is that a small but significant number of Leading-Edge Boomers and members of the Silent Generation, but not a majority of them, have moved to central cities. Given the size of these two generations, even a shift at the margins can have a notable effect.

Where Will Leading-Edge Boomers Move in the Future?

Considerable debate exists about where Leading-Edge Boomers will choose to live in coming years. Some predict they will stay settled in the suburbs. Generally, households headed by someone older than 65 move less than younger ones. The Center for Housing Policy reports that between 2010 and 2011, some 12 percent of households headed by someone 35–39 years of age moved, compared with 2.8 percent of those headed by someone 70–74 years of age.[29] Moreover, according to estimates, 70 percent of the members of the Silent and Greatest generations are living today where they celebrated their 65th birthday.

Many commentators also point to an AARP study[30] reporting that 80 percent of those older than 45 say they want to remain in their homes even when they need assistance. This study, and others like it, is often cited in support of the idea that Leading-Edge Boomers will age in place, not moving from where they are now. Some say they are a generation that moved to the suburbs and will stay there.

Maybe, but "aging in place" is a much misunderstood term. Saying you do not want to move when you finally reach a point where you need some assistance, that you want to continue living independently at home instead of being "institutionalized," is one thing. But this widely shared sentiment says nothing about where you may want to live during the years leading up to the time when you may need assistance.

Reaching one's 60s is a significant life event that often stimulates the urge to move for one reason or another—to fulfill a lifetime dream of the "perfect" home; to move to the city and enjoy urban vitality; or to be near family, friends, and most especially grandchildren. Bateson believes that many of the Leading-Edge Boomers, now in their late 50s and early 60s, who are entering what she calls Adulthood II, are likely to move.

> Throughout human history, place has been a basic element of identity, as basic as family of origin, yet in contemporary America both have been partially set aside. Almost all of the people who turn up in the chapters of this book have initiated their years of Adulthood II with changes in their housing, and I find myself struggling with phrases that combine a sense of grounding with different kinds of mobility. Definitions of home have as much to do with human connections as they do with real estate.[31]

She is not alone in this belief. As Fred Bock wrote in the *New York Times*:

> The boomers are hardly approaching retirement in the manner of their parents. . . . Members of this older generation wanted nothing more to do with work once they retired to what was considered a well-earned respite. . . . Earlier surveys showed that 80 percent [of their parents] wanted to stay right where they were when they retired. Current surveys by AARP . . . and several home-building companies indicate that 60 percent to 80 percent of the G.I. generation's children, the boomers, want to move, especially to less urban areas, when they retire.[32]

Financial pressures may also force many of the Leading-Edge Boomers to move in a search for places with a lower cost of living and less expensive housing.

One caution must be noted, however. As much as Leading-Edge Boomers may want to move, they may be trapped, unable to sell their homes. As noted previously, the Leading-Edge Boomers are, on average, carrying significantly more mortgage debt than preceding generations.

Whereas the members of the Silent and Greatest generations have considerable equity in their homes, many Leading-Edge Boomers refinanced their homes and pulled out equity in the early part of the last decade. In addition, people hoping to move up to a larger home, many of whom are members of the smaller generation X now in their late 30s and early 40s, are finding making such a move harder. They need to sell their own homes in a soft housing market and find financing in a tight mortgage market to buy the Leading-Edge Boomers' homes. The result is that many of the Leading-Edge Boomers find themselves locked into a home they may no longer want, reducing the number of those who might otherwise move.

Those Leading-Edge Boomers who wish to and can move cite a number of factors entering into their decision making:

- Finding a smaller or larger home;
- Being near family and friends;
- Enjoying better weather;
- Finding a more urban location, whether downtown or in a suburban town center;
- Finding a place easier to care for;
- Meeting the need to live more frugally;
- Beginning a new career in a new location;
- Returning to areas where they grew up; and
- Finding a place with better health care or public transportation.

For example, a survey by the MetLife Mature Market Institute and the National Association of Home Builders suggests the following:

> - [W]hen 55+ households choose a particular community, their decision is most often driven by the desire to be close to family and friends. Design and looks also rank high but lost their importance to some extent during the recent economic downturn.
> - Although not cited as often . . . proximity to work is on the rise as a reason for choosing an active adult community. The share citing proximity to work has increased with each survey, from 2% in 2001 to nearly 12% in 2009, suggesting that active adult communities are attracting more residents while they are still in the workforce.[33]

What can be said is that the combination of greater energy and better health, the expectation of a longer life, and freedom from children and their previous jobs, on the one hand, and the new financial constraints, on the other, is a volatile mix. Most likely some of the Leading-Edge Boomers will stay in their homes in the suburbs by choice or by necessity. Others will move to an urban location, be it the central city or a suburban town center. Yet others will move toward the sun as generations before them were doing before the recession. They may be drawn by the affordable housing in those regions in the southwest with high foreclosures, but in doing so they will be moving to places experiencing a changing environment with ever greater challenges from droughts and extreme weather. Overall, the migration to the sun, the south and southwest, although not likely to end, is unlikely to regain its prior strength.

The one certainty is that few Leading-Edge Boomers will be moving from the city to the suburbs. They did so decades ago when they were young and had or were planning to have children.

CHAPTER 4

The Graying of the Suburbs

More than half the members of the 65-plus generations live in the suburbs today.[34] Combined with the fact that many people prefer to remain in their own home for as long as possible or may not be able to sell even if they do wish to move, this suggests that the suburbs will continue to see substantial growth in the population of those over 65 in the decade ahead.

The members of the Silent Generation and the Greatest Generation who are staying in their suburban homes are changing the nature of their communities in many ways. Just by increasing the proportion of the population that is in its 70s, 80s, and 90s, these generations are creating what are in effect "naturally occurring retirement communities," or NORCs. In one sense, this is simply a new name for a pattern that goes back thousands of years, long before our affluent, choice-rich society.

In the past, few people had a choice of where they aged, nor did they want to move from where they had lived their lives, surrounded by family and a community of lifelong friends; often they were even revered and respected as they aged, a phenomenon that is sadly missing today. Blue-collar and lower-income communities have often been much like this as grown children continue living near their parents and are able to help care for them (and are sometimes cared for *by* them). A NORC in this context often meets the needs of people who are cared for in much the same way, as were people in the past.

The pattern of families staying together as the children grow up, however, has become the exception in the United States today. Even in blue-collar and lower-income communities, the younger generation is becoming more mobile, leaving in search of better opportunities or just the adventure of change. This trend creates a challenge for a NORC, a challenge that is particularly acute in the suburbs and rural communities.

Those members of the Silent and Greatest generations who choose to remain in their suburban homes are finding themselves living in places designed for families with young children and cars, communities focused on providing schooling and recreation for children. A church may provide a seniors' center or two, but the major financial investments made by the local government are more likely to be in roads and schools.

The level of support needed by the members of the Greatest Generation is growing. In the suburbs much of the needed care has to be provided in their homes; alternatively, they have to be brought to the service provider. Either way requires cars, vans, and buses (and drivers). This adds to costs as well as to traffic, energy use, and pollution. Although technology is beginning to help provide remote medical monitoring and advice, much of the service needed cannot be provided virtually. Such services include the following:

- Social and recreational programs to keep people from becoming isolated;
- Computer support and training to keep them connected;
- Continuing education programs to keep their minds alert;
- Information and counseling on health, well-being, and finances;
- Home maintenance and referral services to maintain their homes as functional;

- Emergency and preventive health care programs;
- Meal programs for those who cannot or will not cook nutritious meals;
- Shopping for food and clothes; and
- Transportation for all of the above.

Hardest of all to deliver, as the mobility of the Greatest Generation declines, is a sense of community—without which these seniors can become isolated in large, deteriorating homes.

The quality of home maintenance frequently declines in homes lived in by people in their 80s and 90s. This can be caused by dwindling energy and ability, declining finances, or decreasing interest in fixing up the home or in its resale value. A study prepared for the U.S. Department of Housing and Urban Development (HUD)[35] found that homes owned by the elderly appreciated in value at 1 to 3 percent less than the local markets. Often the homes were undermaintained, generally because the owners lacked energy or funds to care for them. The homes were also out of date, either because the owners were content with the homes the way they were or because they had no interest in updating them because they had no plans to sell. "Stayers," the report noted, minimize expenditure on homes as compared to "movers" because they do not intend to sell their home. Beyond the age of 70 or 75, "stayers" are more prevalent. They simply like the house the way it is. The report stated that

> The most direct explanation [for lower home values] is that homes of elderly owners are out-of-date in style and frequently poorly maintained. . . . Health needs or utilities take priority over home remodeling projects, which not only take money and energy, but a tolerance for disruption and dislocation.[36]

A related challenge is the need to modify homes if people become disabled. Today, about 10 million households include at least one member with a disability. The need becomes greater the higher the age of the household; the Center for Housing Policy reports that "while about one-quarter of . . . households aged 65–74 include someone with a disability, the proportion climbs to nearly two-thirds among households with a member 85+."[37] Poverty also increases the likelihood that a household will include someone with a disability; poorer households are more likely to include people with disabilities, up to 44 percent among very-low-income groups, whereas the rates decrease steadily as incomes climb.

This fact suggests that with so many people wishing to age in place, a boom will occur in the home renovation business, especially with renovations targeted to accessibility. Unfortunately, however, many 65-plus households simply cannot afford the needed changes. National programs exist that organize volunteers to help maintain homes for those over 65 and to improve their accessibility, such as Rebuilding Together and Christmas in Action; local programs and nonprofits also attempt to address this issue. However, their impact is limited and insufficient to meet the needs of everyone in most communities.

Another problem that affects a neighborhood more than deteriorating housing is the lack of turnover; as those older than 65 stay in their homes, they keep younger families from moving into the neighborhood. This stalls the traditional "housing ladder," the normal progression of new people coming into a neighborhood with new energy, the desire to fix up and modernize their homes and the community as a whole.

The national housing ladder has already become stagnant as first-time homebuyers have difficulty coming up with a downpayment and bank financing, making it harder for families to sell existing homes and move up. The result is that suburban communities are not experiencing normal and needed regeneration.

Suburban communities are just now coming to grips with this new reality. For instance, the ULI Minnesota District Council, in partnership with the Regional Conference of Mayors and the Center for Housing Policy in Washington, D.C., with support from the Family Housing Fund, has begun exploring ways to help the suburban communities around Minneapolis and St. Paul rethink their housing strategies in light of the increased numbers of people aging in place.

Although every suburb needs to create its own response, the Twin Cities initiative is encouraging communities to find ways to attract more young professionals to balance the age of the population. This option is promising for those suburbs that are close in and linked to urban job centers but problematic for suburbs in the outer ring that are less desirable for young families with two working parents. Nearby suburban town centers, satellites of urbanism, can provide another choice for those over 65, allowing them to move to an urban setting where they may find living easier while staying near their community, family, and friends.

Suburban group homes. One response of some suburban communities is fostering the creation of small group homes. These can provide support and community for their residents in a familiar suburban setting.

Such group homes are challenging to develop because of the need to reconfigure single-family homes for group living and the need to make them accessible to those with physical disabilities. State and local regulatory hurdles, when combined with the cost of rehabilitation, also can make these homes uneconomic. Meeting these challenges and ensuring long-term financial stability are generally beyond the capacity of the future residents, and ongoing support from the local government or a nonprofit is needed. As a result, the development of such group homes is unlikely to become a major trend.

The virtual village. One intriguing and growing response to aging in place, whether in the suburbs or in an urban setting, is something being called the "virtual village." These are springing up in suburbs, central cities, and suburban town centers around the country. They provide in an organized way what neighbors in rural communities often provide informally. This rural neighborhood response to helping people remain in their homes is sometimes known as "tending out."[38]

The virtual village provides a place for members to obtain basic services, such as rides to the doctor; or referrals to local service providers, such as home health care, lawyers, or financial advisers; or help maintaining their homes. Often a small staff organizes a group of volunteers to assist members, who pay an annual fee. Members may also be among the volunteers supporting their peers.

More than 60 such virtual villages have been organized in communities around the country, and new ones are in formation. One of the pioneer villages is Beacon Hill Village in Beacon Hill, Boston, now celebrating its tenth year. Lincoln Park Village serves Chicago's Lake View, Lincoln Park, and Near North communities, while Capitol Hill Village, now five years old, serves the Capitol Hill neighborhood of Washington, D.C. A nonprofit group, Village-to-Village, helps communities establish their own virtual villages and provides a support network for them.

Organizing and maintaining these groups presents challenges; membership can cost as much as $1,000 a year for a household, which leaves many people with little interest in joining a village while they have the energy and ability care for themselves. Consequently, new members are often too frail to be helpful volunteers and are unable to remain in their homes for long. Funding the small staff is a problem, and finding the right balance between fees for membership and services that are high enough to support the program and yet are affordable is difficult. For this reason outside funding is often needed, from the local government, foundations, or the philanthropic community.

Age-restricted communities. Age-restricted communities, suburban housing developments that require at least one member of the family to be at least 55 years of age, were becoming increasingly popular among the Leading-Edge Boomers before the housing crash. Developers like these communities because of the relative ease of obtaining local permits: because the communities do not allow children, local residents do not worry about new housing adding to school taxes or overcrowding existing schools. The market for this housing was strong because many people who wanted to continue living in the suburbs were happy to be free of the noise and disruption from the neighbors' children.

This type of development, along with almost all suburban cul-de-sac development, ended with the housing crash, of course. As one builder said, "The age of age-restricted housing is over." That said, major developers such as Pulte/Del Webb (which builds Sun Cities) continue to build out existing communities, and The Villages, a major age-restricted community north of Orlando, continues to grow successfully. However, major new master-planned communities like Sun Cities and The Villages are unlikely to be started anytime soon.

The developers of less successful age-restricted communities have had several responses. Most dropped prices and offered incentives to buyers in the same way developers of all master-planned communities have, which helped improve sales somewhat. But in a major shift, some developers have been going back to local governments and applying to remove the age restrictions in the hope of broadening the market for their unsold homes. The politics of this move has proved complicated.

Many local citizens are opposing these changes; they do not want more families with children moving in and increasing the pressure on already crowded schools and community facilities in a time of constrained local government finances. Where existing homeowners have already moved into age-restricted communities, they too have resisted the removal of age restrictions out of concern that the qualities and amenities for which they had bargained, especially the absence of children, would be lost.

The fights over these changes have been long and hard, sometimes resulting in litigation. Developers have argued that the only way they can afford to finish these developments is to open the market to younger families. In time, existing homeowners, unhappy as they may be, come to realize that the best way to preserve the value of their homes and communities is to allow the developer to sell the remaining homes to whoever is willing to buy them. Likewise, local citizens have come to see the potential harm that can be caused by the blight of a half-finished community and vacant lots. Slowly, some localities are allowing the age restrictions to be removed.

For instance, Lisa Provost reported in the *New York Times* on June 9, 2011, that the Connecticut towns of Ellington, Tolland, and Southington have all recently approved requests to lift age restrictions for troubled developments. Oxford, Connecticut, settled a lawsuit by agreeing to allow the developer of an 82-unit age-restricted development to replan it as a 140-unit open-age townhouse development in return for an agreement to sell 20 percent of the homes at below-market rates. The same pressure to remove age restrictions on developments is happening in other towns, such as Helmetta, Old Bridge, East Brunswick, and Sayreville in New Jersey.

Among the explanations offered by developers for the lack of sales in age-restricted developments have been that the Leading-Edge Boomers postrecession now either want to continue living in their existing homes or are unable to sell their homes because they are "underwater," that is, worth less than the debt they secure. Other explanations include a new financial conservatism on the part of the boomers and tight mortgage credit.

These explanations, however, may not be the whole story. A shift may well be occurring in the housing market with long-term implications, namely, that Leading-Edge Boomers are not as interested in age-restricted communities as past generations. They are not looking to retire early and are not seeking to isolate themselves among the elderly. Many, in fact, still have children at home and enjoy living around younger families; they may, in fact, find the "nuisance" of children part of the spice of life.

They also need to keep a bedroom available for "boomerang" children, the returning and unemployed gen-Yers bouncing back home from college while they look for work or try to figure out what they want to do with their lives. Multigenerational living is on the rise, as discussed later in this report, and over 20 percent of young adults 25–34 years of age are now living at home, a percentage higher than at any time since 1950.[39] Among those 18–24, a full 40 percent live at home, the overwhelming majority of whom say they are doing so for noneconomic reasons, according to a Pew Research survey.[40] Boomers seem to be closer to their children than they were with their parents, an observation affirmed by conversations with many boomer parents and their children.

Whether a future exists for age-restricted housing cannot yet be predicted, but the market for such housing will remain soft until the overall housing market recovers and, thereafter, more limited than in the past.

CHAPTER 5
Cities for Everyone

Much has been written about the growing number of members of the Leading-Edge Boomers and Silent Generation who have moved from the suburbs to the cities; much is true and some is hyperbole. The empty-nester phenomenon, the couple that sells its suburban home after the children have moved out and buys a condominium in the city, is real and has been occurring; it is hard to quantify, however, and has not involved the majority of suburban households.

Urban living, however, is no longer confined to the central city; a growing number of suburban town centers are developing in metropolitan regions around the country. Although people living in suburban towns are not counted by the census as "city" dwellers, they are voting with their feet and their dollars for a more urban lifestyle.

These "boutique cities," as one ULI member calls them, have become increasingly significant population centers for people of all ages and incorporate retail, office, and commercial development as well as housing. Often they are becoming linked by transit. The people who moved from a suburban cul-de-sac to a suburban town center have benefitted the region by reducing regional congestion and pollution and are now taking local transit or driving less by living closer to jobs, retail, and services.

Aging in the City

In contrast to the suburbs, cities are, or can be, well-designed places for people 65 plus to live in. The traditional urban amenities—better public transit; good health care; a healthier, walkable lifestyle; arts, culture, ongoing education, and libraries; and easy access to services, stores, and human interaction—are all ideal for people of all ages.

The cities to which people over 65 have moved have benefitted greatly from their presence. Members of both the Leading-Edge Boomers and the Silent and Greatest generations who move to cities are often actively employed, support local stores and the arts, can be active volunteers who bring skill and experience to whatever they are involved in, and contribute less to crime rates.

A growing population of people in their late 70s and older, however, presents challenges as well as benefits for a city. At some point people may require support, and just as in the suburbs, this need can put pressure on limited city services at a time of financial constraint. The physical design of the city also may need to be changed and new infrastructure required to better accommodate them.

Redesigning a city to accommodate people in their late 70s, 80s, and older is not necessarily complex or expensive. Simple things like curb cuts, benches at transit stops, access to bathrooms, slower timing of traffic lights to allow time for slower-moving pedestrians to cross, zoning that allows people to rent out portions of their homes, well-maintained sidewalks, and places to walk separate from bicycles all make a large difference for the aging.

The fact that the members of the Silent and Greatest generations are among the most active voters may be seen as either a blessing or a curse for communities, depending on where one stands. Because they vote in disproportionately high percentages, their political impact is magnified. The fact that they are living in the city may not matter on the national political level, but it does shift political weight at the state level to the cities in which they live, a positive development for cities with growing 65-plus populations.

FIGURE 25 Global Population Growth Is Expected to Occur in Urban Areas | PERCENT OF URBAN POPULATION IN MAJOR AREAS OF THE WORLD, 2005 AND 2030

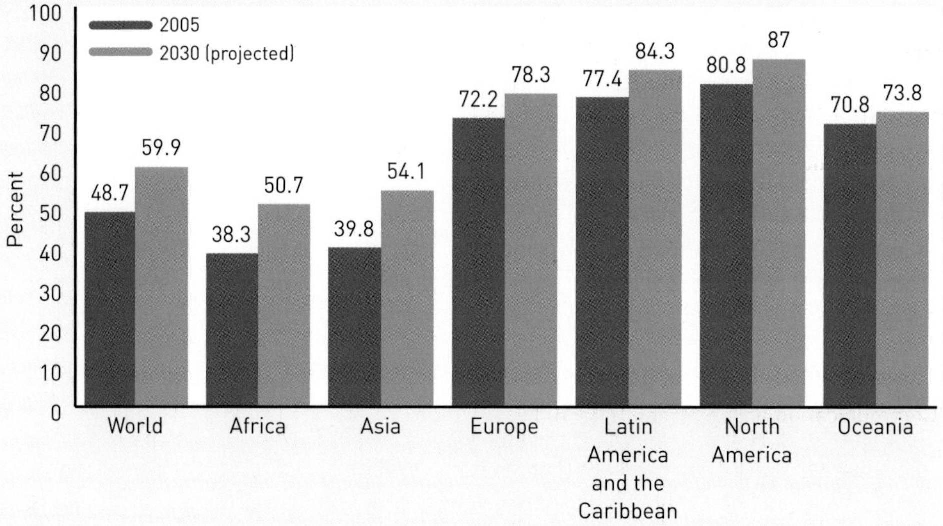

Source: United Nations Department of Economic and Social Affairs, Population Division, 2011.

At the local level, members of the Silent and Greatest generations can have an even greater effect, as they push for services designed for themselves over those designed for younger families with children. Their presence may alter local school politics and cause disputes over parks, libraries, and other "third places" separate from the home and workplace, raising inevitable concerns about whose needs should drive the design and allocation of hours of use.

Designing Cities for Everyone

In 2008 the majority of the world's population lived in cities for the first time in history; by 2030 approximately 3 of every 5 people are expected to live in an urban area. The United Nations projects that virtually all global population growth for decades to come will occur in urban areas, whereas rural areas will lose population.

This rapid global urbanization led the World Health Organization (WHO) in 2006 to study the connection between urbanization and the world's growing 65-plus population, including the aspects of urban life that make cities age-friendly. The study led to the creation of the Global Network of Age-Friendly Cities, the goals of which are as follows:

- To provide technical support and training;
- To link cities to WHO and each other;
- To facilitate the exchange of information and best practices; and
- To ensure that interventions taken to improve the age-friendliness of cities are appropriate, sustainable, and cost-effective.

According to WHO, membership in the network is a public demonstration of commitment by a city to use WHO guidelines to improve the city's "age-friendliness"; it is not an assessment by

WHO that the city does in fact meet the guidelines. To become a member, a city commits to "undertake a process of continually assessing and improving their age-friendliness." The first Conference of Age-Friendly Cities was held in September 2011 in Dublin, Ireland.

In 2007, WHO published *Global Age Friendly Cities: A Guide*. The guide focuses on eight topic areas:

- Outdoor spaces and buildings;
- Transportation;
- Housing;
- Social participation;
- Respect and social inclusion;
- Civic participation and employment;
- Communication and information; and
- Community support and health services.

The topics cover both the hardware of the physical design of a city and the software of social programs. The first three—outdoor spaces and buildings, transportation, and housing—the hardware topics, cover a wide range of sensible and sometimes very basic urban design issues.

WHO also published checklists for each of these topics that include a wide range of matters from the very detailed to the very general. Some items on the checklist are basic good city management, such as keeping public areas clean, safe, and well lit. Others are more targeted, such as providing seating and public toilet facilities, adjusting the timing of traffic lights, and ensuring that sidewalks can accommodate wheelchairs.

Comprehensive as WHO's lists are, notable gaps occur. For instance, no mention is made of ensuring that housing for seniors is located in those parts of a city that have good public transit. The quality of access to public transit can vary widely within a city, and those areas with the best connectivity are often the most valuable and expensive. Adequate housing at a range of prices affordable to people with a range of incomes needs to be provided in transit-rich locations. This goal can be challenging to meet, but isolating moderate- and lower-income people in neighborhoods without easy access to the services they need is harmful and inequitable. Access to adequate public transportation also includes making buses, subways, and trams accessible to everyone with escalators, elevators, and ramps.

Another area missing from the WHO checklists is easy access to "third places" for people to congregate in. The WHO checklists do discuss parks, but more places indoors are needed, such as libraries, seniors' and community centers, restaurants, cafés, and the like, where people can spend time.

Also, as a new generation of people ages, new types of facilities will be needed. As mentioned previously, the Leading-Edge Boomers and members of the Silent Generation are far more active and engaged than any prior generation. Centers with broadband and Wi-Fi access, computer and business centers, support and training for entrepreneurs, and meeting facilities will become more important as the decade progresses.

To date 35 cities around the world are in the WHO network. As of 2011, the only U.S. cities are New York and Portland, Oregon. Among the steps New York is taking are using school buses to transport people to shopping after the buses have finished taking children to school and slowing the timing of traffic lights (this in a city that has the fastest recorded pedestrian pace in the country). New York has also created three "aging improvement districts," neighborhoods where stores commit to put out chairs, use larger signs, and make aisles more accessible for the handicapped. Portland, for its part, is in the process of modifying its planning and zoning rules to accommodate accessible housing.

Atlanta, while not part of the WHO network, is helping create what is being called "Lifelong Communities," which link housing, transit, basic and preventive health care, and easy access to services. Philadelphia is considering revising its zoning code to allow people to rent out rooms on upper floors to provide both income and, possibly, people to support them in living at home.

The kinds of actions being taken by these cities and the additional ones found in the WHO checklists are just as important for suburban town centers as they are for central cities. They also can be useful for suburbs as they look to redevelop themselves, though their car-centric, low-density design makes many of the items harder to implement.

CHAPTER 6

Retirement Housing

SHIFTING MARKETS, NEW APPROACHES

Today some 12 million people are older than 80. As discussed previously, this group will grow rapidly over the decade, adding anywhere between 2.4 million and 4 million to their population, depending on the increase in life expectancy over this period. This represents growth of 20 percent or more in the market for housing communities for seniors, namely those institutions that provide independent and assisted living and full nursing care, or a combination of all three known as a continuing care retirement community. Serving this population are some 50,000 housing communities for seniors.

Yet despite what would seem like a growing market, the industry is virtually in crisis, as one expert put it. Since the beginning of the Great Recession, communities for seniors have faced difficulties in finding new residents to replace those leaving, causing a rising vacancy rate in most communities. The median age at which people move into such a community is rising; only a few years ago, the median was in the late 70s, though new residents can range from their 60s to their 90s, depending on their health and circumstances. Today the average age of new residents has risen to 84.[41]

The rise in age of new residents is caused at least in part by the high cost of retirement housing and the fact that many members of the Silent and Greatest generations have insufficient funds set aside for retirement. Often people are simply deferring payment of the higher cost of housing for seniors as long as possible to save money, even when they have adequate resources. This also may be the reason why signing up a new resident after the initial contact now takes longer.[42]

Another issue facing communities for seniors, and making such properties harder to keep filled, is a growing disaffection with institutional living. No matter how attractive and supportive an institution is, it is still an institution with a need for rules and schedules. Members of the Silent Generation have lived through more of the culture of individualism and self-motivation prevalent since the 1960s and less of the collective spirit that emerged from the Great Depression and experienced by the Greatest Generation. This cultural shift, although gradual now, is likely to become accentuated when the Leading-Edge Boomers reach their late 70s in ten to 15 years.

Some housing communities for seniors are attempting to respond to this disaffection with institutional living by looking for ways to run their communities more flexibly. For instance, some are experimenting with eliminating scheduled meal hours to allow residents to eat on their own schedule. Important as these experiments are, only so much can be done to make a place feel to residents as if they are living on their own while in an institution.

Also affecting communities for seniors is the growth in the number of people living alone by choice. Nathan Heller reports in an article in the *New Yorker* on April 6, 2012, that more than half of U.S. residents are single and nearly a third of all households have just one resident. Importantly, almost 40 percent of women over 65 now live alone.[43] According to research, many people living alone are doing so by choice—and enjoy it. This pattern raises an ethical issue. As Heller says:

> This decade will deliver the first cohort of senior citizens [i.e., the Leading-Edge Boomers] who reached adulthood after the liberalizations of the sixties—the baby boomers are collecting Social Security. As a consequence, we're starting to encounter a group of . . . folks for whom aloneness is a choice, an identity, an exercise in freedom. And the ethics of senior care will change as a result. If Mom has lived alone, successfully and proudly, for four decades, is it socially responsible to move her to a home when she stops remembering to pay her gas bill? Or is it an offense against the person she has spent her adulthood laboring to be?[44]

Although most of the Leading-Edge Boomers will not be confronted with these issues for themselves for another decade or more, they are relevant today for the older members of the Silent Generation, many of whom also have developed the same independent spirit and are living alone by choice.

The popularity of aging in place, the desire of people, especially those older members of the Silent Generation and those in the Greatest Generation, to continue living in their homes as they age and need greater support, is yet another sign of the growing resistance to institutional living and, perhaps, also of the desire to continue living alone. So although the number of people in their late 70s and 80s is growing, the actual market for housing them may shrink during this decade unless new models are found.

Of course, people have plenty of good reasons to move to a community for seniors at some point in their lives. Residents cite personal safety and security, social life, convenience, and the opportunity not to have to move again. They also report that they are more able to stay fit, to continue studying and learning, to eat well, and to enjoy more activities.[45]

FIGURE 26 Very Few 65-Plus Adults Live in Long-Term Care Facilities | PERCENT OF MEDICARE ENROLLEES 65 AND OLDER IN SELECTED RESIDENTIAL SETTINGS, BY AGE GROUP, 2007

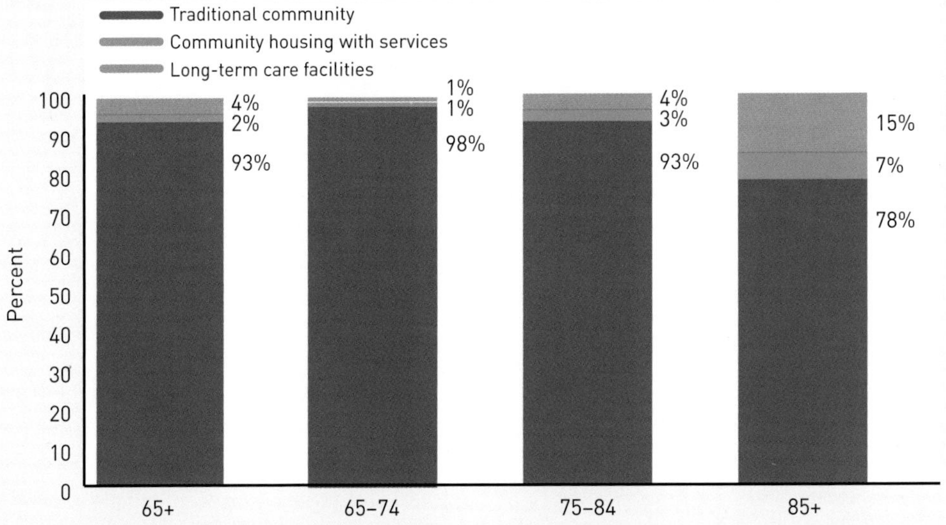

Source: Centers for Medicare and Medicaid Services, Medicare Beneficiary Survey, 2007.
Note: Totals may not equal 100% because of rounding.

Many communities for seniors would like to use these benefits to attract the younger, more active members of the Silent Generation. This would broaden the market for the homes and create healthier communities for all residents. Efforts to achieve this goal, however, have not been successful to date. The primary obstacle has been the age of the current residents; as one sales representative for a seniors' housing community put it, "To attract a younger population, we would need to have a younger population."

The location of new housing communities for seniors may, however, offer the industry an opportunity to broaden this market among the Silent Generation. Today most retirement housing is located in the suburbs, both because they are easier and less expensive places in which to build and because the target market for them when they were built was suburbanites who wished to stay in the suburbs. This market segment will continue to exist during the current decade, but at the same time, another, more urban segment is growing in size.

Locating a property in a walkable urban neighborhood is more likely to attract younger residents, depending on the neighborhood and the design of the development. The right urban location can attract many of those disaffected by suburban institutions and even those who desire to live alone. When residents can walk around a lively neighborhood filled with people of all ages and go to restaurants, stores, and other services on their own as if they were living in their own city apartment, then the sense of living "cooped up" in an institution can be avoided.

An example of a successful multigenerational, urban retirement community is Merrill Gardens/Corydon located in the University District of Seattle, Washington. It is in an urban area near the University of Washington's main campus and comprises 123 independent and assisted-living senior apartments; 103 market-rate apartments, many of which are rented by students; and a liquor store. It was a 2010 ULI Awards for Excellence finalist.

Among the strengths of Merrill Gardens is the way it has combined a residence for seniors with contiguous, independently operated market-rate housing. It provides residents with a home in a walkable, mixed-age neighborhood near a lively university campus. A sign of the strength of this type of mixed-age, urban community is that it fully leased up and met its financial goals even though it opened during the recession.

Merrill Gardens, or communities like it colocated with other types of housing in lively unban, walkable settings, may be the best way to respond to the desires of the members of the Leading-Edge Boomers and the Silent Generation to be more independent and to live alone. Although building in an urban location may be more expensive, the ability to offer an independent, citylike lifestyle may combine the best attributes of what a community for seniors can offer—security, companionship, and the like—with a sense of still living on one's own, often a primary benefit of aging in place.

Greening Housing Communities for Seniors

Retrofitting existing housing developments for seniors can significantly reduce their operating costs and provide a short-term payback on the investment required. Moreover, in addition to financial savings, a successful retrofit brings considerable health and quality-of-life benefits to the 65-plus population.

A study of nine retrofits published last year by the Northwest Energy Efficiency Alliance (NEEA)[46] details how owners were able to achieve energy savings of 50 percent or more and reduce the

An example of a successful multi-generation urban retirement community is Merrill Gardens/Corydon Apartments, located in the University District of Seattle, Washington. *Merrill Gardens and SRM Development*

retrofit cost using various kinds of government, utility, and tax incentives. Accurately predicting payback periods is still hard to do because of insufficient data on particular applications in particular locations; nevertheless, plenty of evidence is available from specific projects to know that green retrofits can produce an attractive financial return on the investment.

The NEEA study also discusses "soft" benefits available, some of which drop to the bottom line. This is especially important for owners of housing properties for seniors; studies by the AARP and others show that people older than 65 have a high degree of environmental awareness, desire environmentally safe products, and understand the health and other benefits of green properties.[47] For this reason, branding a property as green can offer a competitive advantage over other housing properties for seniors that can translate directly into higher absorption and occupancy as well as lower staff turnover. (Skanska, for instance, reports that its LEED Platinum New York headquarters in the newly greened Empire State Building experienced a 16 percent drop in absenteeism after it moved into the building.) A well-designed retrofit can also result in better health outcomes for residents and a more positive attitude among residents and staff, leading, among other things, to better word-of-mouth advertising.

Another "soft" benefit of a green retrofit reported in the NEEA study, and confirmed by the experience of many real estate and financial advisers, is that more investors today are looking for green investments. Although investors may be unsure of the actual "hard" bottom-line benefits, they are concerned that properties that are not green will become uncompetitive, leading them frequently to choose green properties to invest in over those that are not.

Planning the Retrofit

The first step in considering a retrofit is to develop an overall, integrated plan, working with the architects, engineers, contractors, and finance experts. Also important is including those who will operate the new systems, those who work in the building, and even the residents themselves, all of whom significantly affect achieving the designed savings.

Lighting is often an area that offers a quick payback and is a good example of what can be accomplished through a fully integrated approach. Because aging eyes need more light, lighting is particularly important in housing communities for seniors. Lighting technology is evolving at a startling pace, almost weekly, as a lighting controls expert at Cisco put it. To fully benefit from these advances requires consideration of installing not just new lights but also new technologies to run them, such as wireless and computerized controls.

New lighting may also involve redesigning the existing windows, installing light shelves and wells, and adding automatic controls on window coverings to reduce the amount of energy needed for artificial light. Equally important, these changes increase the amount of daylight, which, according to a growing number of studies, can enhance the productivity of the staff as well as the overall mood and health of residents. By combining a number of elements into a complete lighting program, one can achieve shorter payback periods while providing a better, healthier quality of life to the staff and residents.

Other fixes with relatively short payback periods include reducing drafts from doors and windows and new, highly efficient heating, ventilating, and air conditioning (HVAC) systems. New energy-efficient windows installed as part of an integrated lighting retrofit, combined with automatically controlled shades, exterior awnings, and new deciduous trees planted on the south and west sides of buildings, can reduce the size of the new HVAC system required. Once again, looking at the various systems and parts of the building as an integrated whole uncovers areas of savings that are not evident when looking at the parts separately.

After the physical aspects of the retrofit are completed and new equipment installed, the next step is critical: the building must be commissioned. This means that the systems must be tuned and everyone involved in working in and operating the building, including the residents living there, must be trained to use the new systems as designed.

Training alone, however, is insufficient; everyone must be enrolled in the goals of operating the building and its systems as efficiently as possible consistent with convenience and comfort. This is one reason why maintenance personnel, staff, and residents need to be involved from the beginning in designing the retrofit; they are more likely to run the building as intended if they have helped design the retrofit and feel they own the goals from the beginning.

Human behavior affects the efficiency of a building by as much as 40 percent, according to some estimates. The best, most efficient building systems are of little value unless those who operate them want to use them properly and know how to do so. Studying ways to create cultures that support the efficient operation of a building is a recent development. One effort to better understand the human element in building operation and use is the Climate, Buildings and Behavior Project, sponsored by the Garrison Institute and cosponsored by the ULI New York District Council. Over the past several years it has developed a growing library of stories of success and challenges of changing cultures and creating green behaviors in buildings. The project is also compiling reports on the rapidly evolving research into behavioral economics and other fields related to human behavior.

The point is that whenever a housing community for seniors is in need of an update, whether major or minor, or a property needs to be repositioned in the market, a careful focus on all the aspects of sustainable, energy-efficient design is important in achieving long-term financial stability. Also important are the human benefits of a better working environment for the staff and a better quality of life for the residents, which is central to the core mission of any housing community for seniors.

CHAPTER 7

Options, Options, Options

NEW TRENDS OR THE FANCIES OF A FEW?

Leading-Edge Boomers and members of the Silent Generation are discovering a variety of new living arrangements. Although much is uncertain about their future living patterns, one thing seems likely: how and where they live will not simply follow past patterns. They are exploring new ways of living, creating a variety of niche markets each of which may become significant in size, given how large these two generations are. As John Migliaccio, the director of research at the MetLife Mature Market Institute puts it, "Anytime there are so many people you get niches."[48]

How popular these niches will be over the course of the decade remains to be seen. Will they remain small and appeal to only a few, or will they begin to appeal to large numbers in the years ahead? This section reviews a few of the more intriguing options being explored.

College Towns

College towns have been attracting retirees since the mid-1990s. Places like Princeton, New Jersey; Ann Arbor, Michigan; or Athens, Georgia, and dozens of others like them in which colleges or universities are located continue to attract a growing number of well-off retirees with their lovely, relatively quiet walkable neighborhoods. Retirement communities of various kinds are also targeting these towns, offering the perks of on-campus activities to entice residents. Their market includes a combination of retiring college staff and alumni.

The attractions of retiring near colleges and universities are obvious: continuing education, an active arts scene, sporting events, well-known speakers, and an invigorating, youthful environment. Many college towns have excellent health care, especially where a major medical school is part of the campus. Subtler is the illusive attraction of nostalgia when retiring to the town in which one's alma mater is located, though how many alumni actually do move back is unclear.

Another reason why housing for seniors near colleges and universities often succeeds is that people are moving there to be near children and grandchildren who are living in the area. Communities that have university and medical school research facilities and can support the creation of new businesses that capture and build on products coming from the research (called the "eds and meds" phenomenon) are developing stronger local economies than other cities. As more college graduates live in these kinds of thriving centers of research, innovation, and entrepreneurialism, many of their aging parents may well be moving there as well to have more quality time with their grandchildren.

A youthful environment, however, brings with it noise, parties, crowds, and the inevitable bad behavior of many undergraduates. Also, few college towns can boast of easily affordable housing, limiting their attraction to a narrower segment of the market.

Manufactured Housing

Mobile home communities have long been a traditional place to retire for members of the Silent and Greatest generations on limited budgets. The growth of these communities came to a halt with the recession and housing crash and has yet to rebound. Good reason exists to believe that this market may grow substantially in the years ahead, but some obstacles challenge this growth.

Mobile home parks can offer a high quality of living that combines the independence of living in one's own home with a sense of community from the others living in the park. A well-built mobile home is less expensive than a new stick-built home and is made more affordable because the homeowner only pays rent for the site.

One challenge to the future of this market is financial: traditional bank financing for the purchase of a mobile home on a leased site has become hard to obtain. Park owners, retailers, and others are exploring new financing methods to help buyers finance their homes, but the market remains constrained at this time.

Another challenge is the perception of mobile homes as being a low-income housing option. Although some parks fit this image, many more are filled with people of modest but adequate means. Changing this pejorative image is important if parks are to capture the new generation of Leading-Edge Boomers as they enter the market. Boomers are self-conscious about their image and what their housing choices say about them; they are also style conscious and more urban than prior generations. Changing the image of mobile home parks and showing them to be an affordable, stylish, and high-quality place to live, as they often are, is essential to the future of this market.

The manufactured housing industry will have difficulty meeting the growing desire for more urban living. Stiff resistance always greets the attempt to locate new parks, and this resistance is more intense in already developed areas. Not only are sites smaller, hard to find, and expensive for new mobile home parks in established areas, the local resistance is generally very effective. Unfortunately, the fact that mobile homes that meet HUD codes are excluded from local building codes frequently does not prevent local governments from blocking a new park. Negotiating with a community and local activists and helping them understand the nature of the residents in a community for seniors and the quality of the homes and grounds has no easy alternative. All of these challenges, of course, add to the cost that will eventually be borne by the park's residents.

Cohousing and Group Living

The Cohousing Association of the United States describes cohousing as "a type of collaborative housing in which residents actively participate in the design and operation of their own neighborhoods." The concept was imported from Denmark where it was developed in the 1960s.

A cohousing development is typically a group of dwelling units combined with common facilities and a program that encourages social interaction, such as weekly meals cooked and eaten in common, common gardens, and shared babysitting. These developments are set up legally as either a collection of individually owned units with a homeowners association that owns the common facilities or a condominium or housing cooperative.

Most often, a group of families with a common interest in living closely but not communally comes together to plan and build the homes and common facilities. Alternatively, a developer may establish them. At present, more than 200 cohousing projects have been completed or are under development in the United States, according to the Cohousing Association.

Cohousing advocates are now promoting it as a promising lifestyle for people over 65. Some see benefits to seniors-only communities, and others are encouraging multigenerational communities.

Over time, however, issues of ensuring long-term affordability and providing increasing levels of care for residents are likely to arise. How cohousing communities deal with these issues will determine whether the communities are sustainable. Arguably, residents can provide support for one another, although mutual interdependence can be problematic where all residents are of roughly the same age. This is one reason some advocates recommend multigenerational communities, which has the advantage of allowing residents to also provide daycare or babysitting services.

Cohousing provides a sense of community and can provide high-quality housing for those who can afford it. The complexity of organizing a basic cohousing community, providing services for an aging population, and meeting long-term costs and ensuring financial stability suggests that cohousing is likely to remain a relatively small niche in the years ahead.

Multigenerational Living

A multigenerational household is generally defined as one that contains at least two adult generations or a grandparent and at least one other generation. This classic living arrangement fell out of favor in the United States during the last century as increased social and economic mobility allowed people to live independently. Recently, it is coming back into favor.

The Center for Housing Policy reports that "According to recent census data, a relatively small segment of the population (5.1 million households, 4.4 percent) has three or more generations living under the same roof. But the number is rising faster than households overall."[49]

For instance, in 1900, 57 percent of age 65-plus adults lived in a multigenerational household. By 1990, this number had dropped to just 17 percent. By 2010, however, the number of adults in multigenerational households had grown to 20 percent.[50] As a percentage of all households, multigenerational households have risen from a low of 12.1 percent in 1980 to 16.1 percent in 2009.[51]

Several factors are contributing to this trend. Clearly the recession is causing families to move back in together, whether young college "bounce backs" or parents moving in with adult children. This is not the only reason, however; household size, which had been falling since the 1950s, began increasing as early as 2005, well before the recession. This trend suggests that another driver of multigenerational living is the large number of Asian and Latino immigrant families who arrived over the course of the recent wave of immigration and brought with them a tradition of living in multigenerational households.

How far this trend will go depends in part on the economy. If high unemployment rates continue, more families, by choice or by necessity, probably will choose to live together. Immigration has slowed to a standstill as a result of the poor economy, reducing its impact on this trend; when jobs come back, however, immigration will as well. Multigenerational living also depends on how many younger families may want to have Mom and Dad move in to make caring for them easier and less expensive. All these factors together indicate that multigenerational living does not seem likely to become as common as it was in 1900. That said, the number of multigenerational households is likely to increase steadily through the remainder of the decade.

Should the housing industry begin to respond to this renewed trend? Should the size of new homes and apartments be larger, or should they have more bedrooms or independent living quarters? Most probably, the response should be cautious. Many large suburban homes are already available for larger families; demand for them is currently modest and is likely to remain so for some years. Thus, the need to build suburban homes for multigenerational households is not great, though the existing homes may require reconfiguration to provide some privacy and independence for different adult groups within the household.

The more difficult challenge is how to provide adequate housing for multigenerational households in urban areas. Townhouses are appropriate, but apartments are more problematic. Apartments can be built large enough to accommodate mixed-generation families and can be configured to provide a sense of independence; this, however, is expensive and narrows the market for these units. If multigenerational living is a response to constrained finances, then new

FIGURE 27A Multigenerational Households Have Rebounded in Popularity | U.S. POPULATION LIVING IN MULTIGENERATIONAL HOUSEHOLDS, 1940–2009 (MILLIONS)

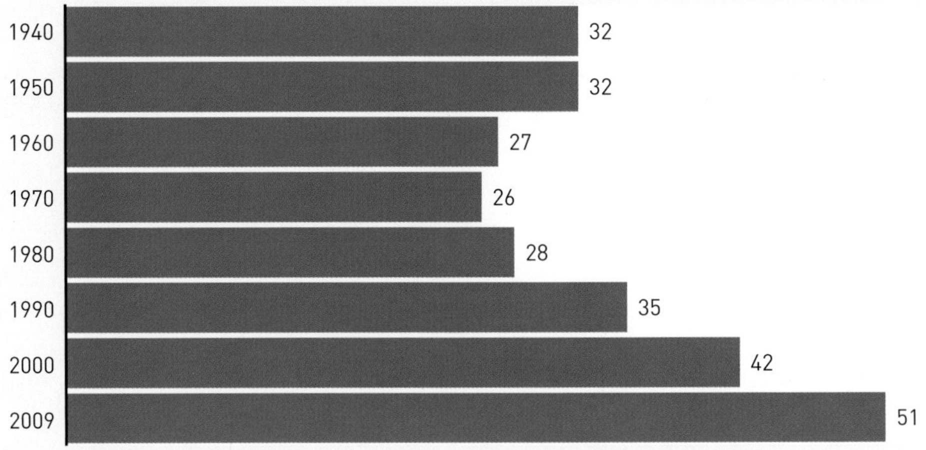

Source: Pew Research Center, 2011.

FIGURE 27B Multigenerational Households Have Rebounded in Popularity | SHARE OF U.S. POPULATION LIVING IN MULTIGENERATIONAL HOUSEHOLDS, 1940–2009

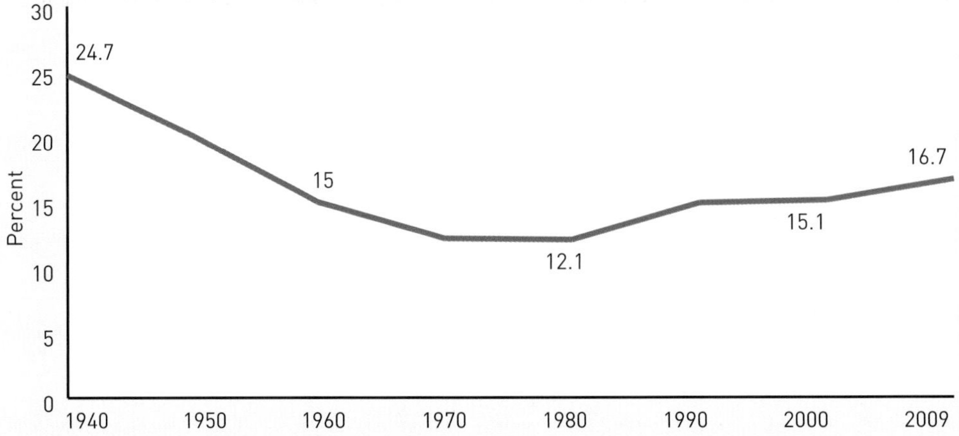

Source: Pew Research Center, 2011.

FIGURE 28 One-Fourth of Asian Americans Live in Multigenerational Households | SHARE OF POPULATION IN MULTIGENERATIONAL FAMILY HOUSEHOLD, BY RACE/ETHNICITY, 2008 (%)

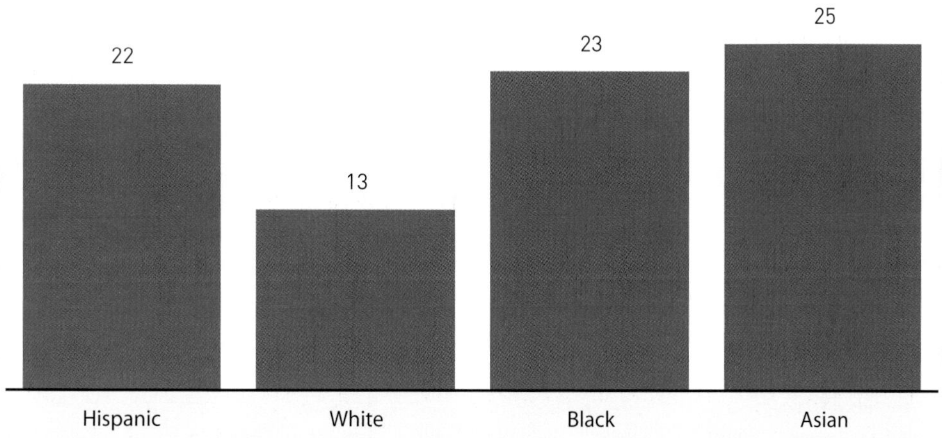

Source: Pew Research Center, 2010.
Note: Hispanics are of any race. White, black, and Asian include only non-Hispanics.

apartments are not likely to be a practical solution, although combining apartments in an existing building may be feasible for some families.

Affinity Retirement Communities

A trend emerging among retirement communities is the creation of what are known as "affinity" communities. They target retirees with a common interest or lifestyle. Some experts believe that this trend will grow as Leading-Edge Boomers begin moving to retirement communities; the boomers, they reason, have more often defined themselves by their interests and leisure pursuits than prior generations.

Examples include golf and tennis communities, as well as ones for RV lovers, tai chi enthusiasts, art or music aficionados, or even nudists. The number of university-based retirement communities targeted at alumni, for example, has doubled in the last decade. Andrew Carle, the founding director of the senior housing administration program at George Mason University, says that "These 'affinity communities' are one of the biggest trends in retirement living."[52]

The ability to be culturally sensitive is especially important to certain groups, such as Asian Americans or the lesbian, gay, bisexual, and transgender (LGBT) communities. Sensitivity to colors, feng shui, and cultural etiquette are important for elderly Asian Americans. For the LGBT community, being around others open to the gay lifestyle and being free from those who may be uncomfortable with it provides a more open, healthier environment in which to live. Staffing these communities with people appropriate for the particular community can make a large difference in the quality of life for residents.

Costs for these communities run the gamut from moderate to very expensive. Whether a particular community remains sustainable is hard to predict; although they may be very attractive to a particular group of people, that group may be quite narrow, thus making filling empty apartments or homes a slow process whether at the initial opening of the community or over time as units become available. For some residents the narrow focus of activities also may become tiresome, and they may leave for wider pastures. As a result, not all these communities have succeeded in becoming sustainable over time.

Some of these affinity communities are NORCs, occurring naturally as people come together in neighborhoods with others like them. Examples are Provincetown, Massachusetts, where many members of the LGBT community are living, or the ethnic neighborhoods of communities like Arlington, Virginia, and the various Chinatowns in New York, San Francisco, and elsewhere.

Universal Design

Universal design seeks to create environments, objects, and systems that can be used by as many people as possible and is intended to create places for people of all ages and abilities. It is also of growing importance in the design of places intended for occupancy by people with disabilities now or in the future and for places that such people may visit, such as the homes of their children and grandchildren. In fact, given that almost everyone is likely to experience a severe if temporary disability at one time in their life, making all homes universally accessible makes fundamental good sense.

Universal design is especially important for those who want to age in place, which all too often means continuing to live in homes designed for young, healthy families with children. These homes need things like stairs, doorknobs, grab bars, counter heights, and door widths to be added, redesigned, or replaced. Some of these items are easy to change whereas others require a larger investment. One challenge, then, is to find affordable and effective ways to retrofit homes.

The growth of the 65-plus population is but one reason for the whole housing industry to incorporate adaptability into the development of all new housing, whether single family or multifamily. A new home does not need the expense of all the features a frail or disabled person would require; what is needed is a design that allows adding these features easily when they are needed later.

CHAPTER 8

Conclusion

THE ROLE OF GOVERNMENT

Americans are firm believers in the importance of individuals caring for themselves. Alongside this strain of individualism runs a deep theme of communitarian cooperation, whether it is neighbors raising a barn on the frontier or a bake sale to raise funds for someone burned out of his or her home.

American individualism is reflected in the number of people who want to stay in their homes as long as possible and the growing number of them who live alone by choice. The day comes for many, however, when they simply are unable to fully care for themselves. For the fortunate, their families are their first line of support. After that, and often in concert with their families, are churches, local groups of volunteers, nonprofits, and the for-profit housing community for seniors.

What happens, however, when the needs of people in a community overwhelm the care that can be provided? At this point government needs to enter the picture with its greater resources and organizing capacity. Our governments, be they local, state, or federal, are, after all, how we organize ourselves to provide support when all other means fail.

For the rapidly growing population of those over 65 in the United States, as in countries elsewhere, governments can and must play a growing role if these populations are to receive the level of care they need and to which they are entitled as members of our communities. The role that it is appropriate for government to play naturally varies at different levels and is a focus of much political dispute.

The Local Role

A recent survey of local governments found that they expect their greatest challenges to be providing transportation and housing. The greatest concern they expressed was their inability to obtain the funding needed for these and other necessary services.[53] In addition to the always limited nature of local resources that must be stretched to cover a wide range of needs is the resistance suburban voters may show to spending funds in the amounts necessary to provide adequate care.

That said, local governments can do many things, even with limited funds. They can, for instance, create or support local centers for seniors where services provided range from health and wellness to business support and development, computer classes, adult learning programs, arts programs, and exercise and rehabilitation.

Supporting the creation of one or more "virtual villages" is another way cash-strapped local governments can indirectly deliver support, providing some funding and organizing support, and offer a range of services for those aging in place. Local governments can also encourage the creation of homes for seniors in existing large family homes.

Local governments also need to focus on zoning and building codes. Allowing group homes, accessory dwelling units, and easier zoning and building code reviews for seniors' housing communities can go a long way to reducing their costs and providing affordable housing for seniors.

Other types of zoning and building code changes that are important include permitting more multifamily development and creating single-room occupancy homes for those members of the Leading-Edge Boomers and Silent Generation who wish to live alone. Enforcing the requirements of the Fair Housing Act and Americans with Disabilities Act and encouraging universal design are also low-cost actions a local government can take.

Providing transportation for those who cannot drive their own cars can range from the expensive to the very inexpensive. Special vans and buses can be expensive to buy and operate, but ensuring that existing transit is accessible and that local routes are senior-friendly can be less expensive. As new equipment is acquired, making it senior-friendly does not add much expense. Benches and shelters can be expensive to install but are important. A simple, inexpensive, but important change can be slowing the timing of lights at crosswalks. Other things local governments can do are listed in the WHO age-friendly cities guide discussed previously.

Where resources are available, the local government, working with local for-profit and nonprofit developers and home contractors, can help low-income owners (and landlords) with retrofits by providing technical assistance, volunteer labor, and funding. This help can also be provided for retrofitting homes to make them usable as group homes.

Finally, local governments need to be careful not to allow property taxes on homes owned by those over 65 on limited, fixed incomes to rise beyond what they can afford. This only forces them to leave or to choose between paying the taxes or paying for their daily needs or health care.[54]

The State Role

States place a heavy regulatory burden on housing for seniors and create significant liabilities that property owners must account for and insure against and that ultimately residents must pay for. Important as careful regulation may be for an industry that provides such a basic need for a population that is often vulnerable and less able to protect itself from the unscrupulous, doing so without unduly increasing the costs borne by the elderly is also important. No one right way to do this exists, but the growing pressure of rising costs and falling resources will require state regulators, advocates for the elderly, and industry representatives to work together to find less expensive but equally effective ways of regulating housing for seniors.

The Federal Role

The role of the federal government (along with state governments) is basically to provide resources and program guidelines to local governments and to finance the development of housing communities for seniors with low or moderate incomes. Unfortunately, the federal and state affordable housing programs are already heavily oversubscribed and today meet the needs of only one in every four eligible households, regardless of age.[55]

Sadly, today the federal government and most state governments are pulling back support for affordable housing as a result of both federal budget deficits and lack of political support for funding housing programs. This trend is part of a broader cutback in federal funding for the provision of all kinds of services at the federal, state, and local levels, a thinning out of the national safety net. Hard as this is on the millions of low- and moderate-income households eligible and in need of subsidized housing and other services, it is especially hard on people in the Silent and Greatest generations with limited abilities and few places to turn for help.

The combination of the Leading-Edge Boomers reaching 65 with expectations of a longer life than ever before and the fact that many of the Silent and Greatest generations are running through their limited retirement savings, on the one hand, and a continuing reduction in federal and state resources for housing subsidies, on the other, is leading to a coming crisis in U.S. housing for those over 65. Over the next decade, localities will face great pressure to keep those living in their communities sheltered and cared for and to fill the gap the federal and state governments are leaving.

Former HUD secretary Henry Cisneros captures the challenge and opportunity well in his recent book when he says:

> [T]he population of older people in our country is now becoming so large that strategies of improving existing homes, of incorporating universally useful features in new homes, of building thoughtful new communities, and of retooling existing neighborhoods must be broadly integrated into our community building strategies at the local level across the United States. This initiative is not a matter of creating homes for seniors as acts of obligation although, as a nation, we certainly owe a debt of gratitude that would make obligation reason enough. Rather, it is in the interest of our nation that we all benefit from the longevity dividend, that we secure the best quality of life for all our citizens, and that we live up to the ideal that every single person can contribute to the nation's well-being over the span of an entire lifetime.[56]

There is no way of knowing how the politics of aging will unfold in the years ahead, but it is hard to imagine that millions of moderate- and low-income members of the Silent and Greatest generations will be left homeless. This issue will become more acute a decade from now, when the greater number of the Leading-Edge Boomers approach their 80s. Where the funds to care for them will come from, how the care will be provided, and how well they will be provided, are major, looming questions for all levels of government in the decade ahead.

We may be moving into the next great American housing crisis. Although signs at this time are not promising, one must keep in mind that those over 65 wield significant political power at all levels of government. They traditionally vote in far greater numbers than younger people, and they are better organized thanks to organizations like the AARP. Already over 50 percent of all federal benefits flow to those in the Silent and Greatest generations and are being largely protected in the current battles over the long-term federal budget, whereas payments for education and child care services are being cut. Stretched as the members of the Silent and Greatest generations are financially, their financial situation is better than that of generation Y. This young generation is facing the worst financial future of any generation since the Great Depression and anticipating bearing the burden of caring for all three of the 65-plus generations. How federal and state funding will be divided among generations in an era of diminished federal resources will be a dominant political and policy struggle of the coming decade and beyond.

Endnotes

1 Landon Y. Jones coined the term "baby boom generation" in his 1980 book, *Great Expectations: America and the Baby Boom Generation* (New York: Coward, McCann and Geoghegan).

2 Human Mortality Database, United States of America, Complete Data Series, Population size (1-year), University of California, Berkeley, and Max Planck Institute for Demographic Research, Rostock, Germany, http://www.mortality.org/cgi-bin/hmd/country.php?cntr=USA&level=1 (accessed August 20, 2012).

3 Journalist Tom Brokaw coined the term "Greatest Generation" for the generation that grew up during the Great Depression and fought in World War II.

4 Human Mortality Database, *op. cit.*

5 The term "Silent Generation" comes from a November 5, 1951, cover story in *Time* magazine about those born during the Great Depression and World War II.

6 Human Mortality Database, *op. cit.*

7 Mary Catherine Bateson, *Composing a Further Life: The Age of Active Wisdom* (Toronto: Alfred A. Knopf, 2010), 11.

8 Ibid., 12.

9 Ibid., 13–14.

10 AARP, *Approaching 65: A Survey of Baby Boomers Turning 65 Years Old* (Washington, D.C.: AARP, 2010), 4.

11 Bateson, *op. cit.*, 8.

12 William Frey, "Age," in *State of Metropolitan America* (Washington, D.C.: Brookings Institution Metropolitan Policy Program, 2010), 78.

13 Nicolas P. Retsinas, "China: Who Will Take Care of the Elderly?" *Urban Land*, February 29, 2012, http://urbanlandstaging.uli.org/Articles/2012/Mar/RetsinasChina.

14 Statistics Bureau, "Population," in *Statistical Handbook of Japan 2011* (Tokyo: Statistical Bureau, Ministry of Internal Affairs and Communications), http://www.stat.go.jp/english/data/handbook/c02cont.htm#cha2_2

15 U.S. Census Bureau, "2008 National Population Projections," http://www.census.gov/population/www/projections/2008projections.html.

16 Henry Cisneros, Margaret Dyer-Chamberlain, and Jane Hickie, *Independent for Life: Homes and Neighborhoods for an Aging America* (Austin: University of Texas, 2012), 8.

17 George S. Masnick, Zhu Xiao Di, and Eric S. Belsky, "Emerging Cohort Trends in Housing Debt and Home Equity," Joint Center for Housing Studies, Harvard University, Cambridge, Mass., 2005, 2, 3.

18 Ibid., 13.

19 "Seniors Rise in Work Force after Slump," *Wall Street Journal*, March 27, 2012, http://online.wsj.com/article/SB10001424052702303816504577303640088978010.html.

20 Richard Fry, D'Vera Cohn, Gretchen Livingston, and Paul Taylor, *The Rising Age Gap in Economic Well-Being: The Old Prosper Relative to the Young* (Washington, D.C.: Pew Research Center, 2011).

21 Barbara Lipman, Jeffrey Lubell, and Emily Salomon, *Housing an Aging Population: Are We Prepared?* (Washington, D.C.: The Center for Housing Policy, 2012), 1.

22 Fry, Cohn, Livingston, and Taylor, *op. cit.*, 1.

23 Ibid., 2.

24 Ibid.

25 U.S. Census Bureau, Current Population Survey, 2010 Annual Social and Economic Supplement, Table A1. Marital Status of People 15 Years and Over, by Age, Sex, Personal Earnings, Race, and Hispanic, 2010.

26 Kelvin Pollard and Mark Mather, "Slower Growth of U.S. Retirement Destinations Linked to Economic Downturn," Population Reference Bureau, http://www.prb.org/articles/2010/censusdata.aspx.

27 Frey, "Age," *op. cit.*, 78.

28 Ibid.

29 Lipman, Lubell, and Salomon, *op. cit.*, 13.

30 MetLife Mature Market Institute, *MetLife Report on Aging in Place 2.0: Rethinking Solutions to the Home Care Challenge* (New York: Metropolitan Life Insurance Co., 2010), 5.

31 Bateson, *op cit.*, 36.

32 Fred Brock, "Baby Boomer's Second Act," *New York Times Great Homes and Destinations*, http://www.nytimes.com/ref/realestate/greathomes/GH-Retire.html.

33 MetLife Mature Market Institute and National Association of Home Builders (NAHB), *Housing Trends Update for the 55+ Market: New Insights from the American Housing Survey* (New York: Metropolitan Life Insurance Co., 2011), 3.

34 Lipman, Lubell, and Salomon, *op. cit.*, 14.

35 David Rodda and Satyendra Patrabansh, "The Relationship between Homeowner Age and House Price Appreciation." Report by Abt Associates for the U.S. Department of Housing and Urban Development, Office of Policy Development and Research, Washington, D.C., 2005.

36 Ibid., 3.

37 Lipman, Lubell, and Salomon, *op. cit.*, 1.

38 "Tending out" is a lovely phrase common in rural Maine communities, and according to Nancy Hamilton, an expert in this service, it is used to carefully distinguish those who are helping to care for someone ill or aging in the neighborhood from those who are *responsible for* the care recipient.

39 Kim Parker, "The Boomerang Generation; Feeling OK about Living with Mom and Dad," Pew Research Center, March 15, 2012, 2.

40 Ibid., 6.

41 Norma B. Coe and April Yanyuan Wu, "Financial Well-Being of Residents in Senior Housing and Care Communities: Evidence from the *Residents Financial Survey*" (Center for Retirement Research at Boston College, Chestnut Hill, Massachusetts, April 2012).

42 Another possible explanation is a phenomenon called "compressed morbidity." This term means that more people appear to be remaining healthier longer while at the same time starting to decline in health much closer to their ultimate death. If true, this trend not only will continue to push the age at which people enter housing for seniors back but also will shorten the period in which people become among the frail elderly requiring more intensive—and expensive—care.

43 Lipman, Lubell, and Salomon, *op. cit.*, 1.

44 "The Disconnect: Why Are So Many Americans Living by Themselves?," *New Yorker*, April 16, 2012, http://www.newyorker.com/arts/critics/books/2012/04/16/120416crbo_books_heller.

45 Lipman, Lubell, and Salomon, *op. cit.*, 13.

46 New Buildings Institute, *A Search for Deep Energy Savings: NEEA's Study of Existing Building Energy Efficiency Renewals*, prepared for the Northwest Energy Efficiency Alliance (August 2011).

47 Joyce Polhamus, "In Search of New Models for Seniors' Housing," *Urban Land* (September 2008), 218–220.

48 Catey Hill, "A Retirement Made for You (and People Just Like You), The New Trend in Retirement Communities: Shared Interests, Cultures or Lifestyles," SmartMoney.com, http://www.smartmoney.com/retirement/planning/niche-retirement-homes-for-likeminded-people-1308694206127/.

49 Lipman, Lubell, and Salomon, *op. cit.*, 3.

50 Paul Taylor et al., "The Return of the Multi-Generational Family Household," Pew Research Center Publications, March 18, 2010.

51 Rakesh Kochhar and D'Vera Cohn, *Fighting Poverty in a Bad Economy, Americans Move in with Relatives* (Washington, D.C.: Pew Research Center, 2011).

52 Hill, "Retirement," *op. cit.*

53 Lipman, Lubell, and Salomon, *op. cit.*, 17.

54 See Ron Littlefield and Robert H. McNulty, "Local Community Action," in Cisneros et al., "*Independent for Life*," page 159, for a good discussion of actions local governments can take.

55 Lipman, Lubell, and Salomon, *op. cit.*, 17.

56 Cisneros et al., "*Independent for Life*," 17–18.

About the Author

John K. McIlwain is the senior resident fellow, ULI/J. Ronald Terwilliger Chair for Housing at the Urban Land Institute in Washington, D.C. An author, speaker, and former lawyer, McIlwain brings more than 35 years of experience in the fields of housing, housing investment, and development of sustainable housing.

As the senior resident fellow for Housing, McIlwain's responsibilities include leading ULI's research efforts to seek and promote affordable housing solutions in the United States and other nations, including development and housing patterns designed to create sustainable future environments for urban areas. McIlwain is immediate past chairman of the Center for Housing Policy and a past president of its affiliate, the National Housing Conference, an umbrella organization in Washington for low-income and affordable housing issues. He is also a past president of the National Housing and Rehabilitation Association.

Prior to joining the ULI staff, McIlwain founded and served as senior managing director of the American Communities Fund for Fannie Mae in Washington, D.C. The American Communities Fund was a venture fund founded by Fannie Mae and dedicated to investing in hard-to-finance affordable housing. In this capacity, he was responsible for structuring, underwriting, and closing equity investments in more than $700 million of residential and neighborhood retail developments in lower-income communities around the country. He also structured, negotiated, and closed more than $100 million in historic tax credit and inner-city equity investments funds with Lend Lease, AEW Capital Management, and the Community Development Trust. Before taking that position, he was president and chief executive officer of the Fannie Mae Foundation.

Before joining Fannie Mae, McIlwain was the managing partner of the Washington law offices of Powell, Goldstein, Frazer and Murphy, where he represented a broad range of clients in the single-family and multifamily housing areas.

McIlwain also served as executive assistant to the assistant secretary for housing/federal housing commissioner at the U.S. Department of Housing and Urban Development. He began his career in housing as assistant director for finance and administration and deputy director of the Maine State Housing Authority.

He currently serves on the board of directors of the Community Preservation and Development Corporation, the advisory board of Greenline Ventures LLC New Markets Tax Credit Funds, the board of directors of the International Housing Coalition, and the editorial board of *The TOD Line*—the New York and Connecticut transit-oriented development newsletter.

McIlwain received a law degree from New York University where he worked for the *NYU Law Review* and was a John Norton Pomeroy Scholar. He received a BA, cum laude, from Princeton University.